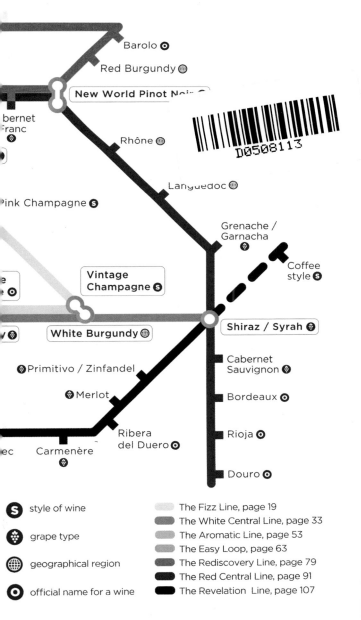

Barolo ⊙

Red Burgundy ⊕

New World Pinot Noir ⊙

bernet Franc ⊛

Rhône ⊕

Languedoc ⊕

Pink Champagne ⊛

Grenache / Garnacha ⊛

Coffee style ⊛

Vintage Champagne ⊛

White Burgundy ⊕

Shiraz / Syrah ⊛

⊛ Primitivo / Zinfandel

Cabernet Sauvignon ⊛

⊛ Merlot

Bordeaux ⊙

Ribera del Duero ⊙

Rioja ⊙

ec Carmenère ⊛

Douro ⊙

Legend

⊛ style of wine

⊛ grape type

⊕ geographical region

⊙ official name for a wine

D0508113

The Pocket Guide to Wine

featuring **The WineTubeMap**®

Nikki Welch

BIRLINN

First published in 2014 by
Birlinn Limited
West Newington House
10 Newington Road
Edinburgh
EH9 1QS

www.birlinn.co.uk

Reprinted 2015

ISBN: 978 1 78027 144 6

British Library Cataloguing-in-Publication Data

A catalogue record for this book
is available from the British Library

Designed and typeset by Mark Blackadder

Printed and bound by Livonia, Latvia

Contents

Introduction

When I first decided I wanted to work in the wine world, I had no real idea what that would entail – I just liked wine.

Having lived abroad, in France and Spain, I had acquired a taste for a glass of something nice with my lunch or dinner and I wanted to find out more. I very quickly realised that, apart from red, white, rosé or sparkling, I knew nothing about the names, flavours and history of wines, and so I quickly applied myself to learning everything I could by tasting as much as I could.

What amazed me was how little it took for me to be able to tell the difference between wines – to spot a Viognier from a Sauvignon Blanc – without any real technical knowledge. I was impressing my friends, family and myself with my new-found knowledge, and all I had done was tasted a few wines!

This book is my attempt to share that feeling of discovery and potential that wine offers without getting bogged down in the detail. It's easy to be put off trying new wines by the sheer volume of bottles on the shelf or on a restaurant's wine list. This book will help you discover some new favourites.

Glossary

S Style of wine

Some wines fall together in logical categories. For example, a certain style of wine that is common to many regions and shares techniques of production (Pink Fizz, for example), a name for a technique of winemaking which is used across the world and gives the wine a certain style (like Traditional Method), or a term used for a specific type of wine which technically means something different (like Moscato).

🍇 Grape type

Most of the grapes used in making wine are different varieties from the same grape family. These days it has become more common to list the name of the grape or grapes in a wine on the label, whereas before the label was more likely to feature the region and/or appellation (*see Official name below*).

The flavour and style of a wine made from a certain grape can change dramatically depending on the climate, the soil and the winemaking techniques, although you can almost always taste the family resemblance.

Geographical region

For a number of reasons, the region where a wine is made can have a huge impact on its style. The landscape and climate will influence the flavour and texture of a wine. However, the regions highlighted on the WineTubeMap tend to reflect the historical style of the wines made there, with more focus on the grapes and techniques used. Within that region there will be a number of different wines, but they will share similarities.

Official name

One of the most confusing things about wine is that it can be named in so many ways. In Europe the names and styles of many local wines are protected by legislation known as appellations. For any appellation there is a set of rules defining the relevant grape variety, geographical boundaries, type of vineyard management and winemaking techniques. If you see AOC (French), DOC or DOCG (Italian), DO (Spanish), DOCP (Portuguese) or QbA or QmP (German) on a label it refers to the appellation. Sadly it doesn't always guarantee quality.

The WineTubeMap®

I'm assuming the very fact you've got this book means you want to discover more about wines, albeit for one of many reasons. Maybe it's just for the pleasure of knowing more about wine, or to make sure you're getting the best value for money when shopping. Or maybe it's to make choosing a wine less daunting when you're in a restaurant with your friends, boss or potential new love interest. It might also be to enhance your flourishing culinary skills. Most likely it's a mixture of all these things.

Whatever the case, there are a number of options available to you. Either you can go and learn about wine (and there are a plethora of beginner courses out there) by learning how it's made and then taking some time to discover the regions, or you can try to teach yourself by taking every available opportunity to taste different wines and finding out more as you go. The problem with the former is that it can take a lot of time and effort, and the problem with the latter is that there are so many wines out there that it can be virtually impossible to know where to start!

After tasting wine with hundreds of people at events, and with all my friends and family asking me questions about what they should be trying, I realised that what people wanted most of all was a recommendation along the lines of 'if you like that, you should try this . . .' And so I, with a lot of help and input from others, have put together the biggest wine recommender I could. The idea is that you can start off with a wine you know and like and then move one step in a number of directions to something similar but a bit different, and then take another step each time, knowing that you're not going to be drinking wine a million miles away from where you started. You can also move gradually from red to white, oaked to unoaked, still to sparkling.

I ended up with a kind of tube map – a set of 'lines', defined mostly by flavour, which interlink at certain points. On these lines are 'stations', each of which represent a type of wine, be it a grape, an appellation or a style. Some of the stations are straightforward; others are like busy interchanges where you could head off in a number of different directions.

Of course, every wine is unique and the same grape from different climates, winemakers and vintages can taste completely different. Where there is a big change of style from region to region I've tried to break them down, but sometimes it makes sense for them to be grouped together and in those cases I've highlighted some of the major styles.

It's worth noting that I've not just stuck to grape types: for some areas it is easy to do, but for others the name of the appellation or even a broader category seemed more appropriate, in the pursuit of something useable and relevant. So, for example, Pink Fizz became a category to encompass sparkling rosé wines from all over the world.

I hope you can use the WineTubeMap and head off on your own voyage of discovery. However, if you need some guidance and help along the way, there are descriptions of each of the stations and lines, as well as some highly recommended routes. The book is laid out with an introduction to each line and then all the stations are grouped together so you can see them in context. Each station entry includes some information about the wines, plus top tips and ideas for food matches.

Of course, there isn't a science to doing this and some wines could sit in one of two or three places. The WineTubeMap is based on my own perception, tested out with patient friends and family – who obviously hate having to come round and taste wines!

So, have a play with it, and at the end of the book I have some more advanced suggestions, for when you feel like you want to head off-piste!

○ Start by finding a wine you like.
○ Look at the line or lines it features on.
○ Does the sound of that line appeal? If so, try the next wine along from your favourite, and if you like that try the next one, and so on. If you go too far then try going in the other direction.
○ Another tip is to look at all the stations where lines cross and try all of those wines – if you like them you can then head off on some new journeys.
○ If you're looking for a gift, buy someone who loves a certain wine something from the next station along – for example if you know they like Shiraz you could buy them a Languedoc wine. You'll expand their horizons while at the same time showing off your new-found wine knowledge.

Making the Most of Wine

Wine isn't just a flavoured drink that gets you merry; it's a stimulus for all of our senses. With most advice being to drink less and drink better, how can you squeeze every drop of value out of the wine that you do buy, especially when there's pressure on the bank balance? It's obvious really: use your senses. The smell of wood fires brings to mind cosy autumn days; the feeling of sand between your toes is a reminder of holidays gone by, and the taste of a certain dish can remind you of the person with you when you first tasted it. We rely so much on our senses, so it's logical to carry that through to your wine choices.

VISION
Bottle
Wine labels play a huge part in your choice of wine: you're looking for something that attracts you stylistically, and as with everything this is very personal. Whatever you're buying you want it to look undamaged and be able to read what's inside – beyond that it's down to your choice. Some people love a bit of tradition: swirly calligraphy and a picture of a chateau. Others like a more modern look, such as a pun or a comedy label. Wine companies invest heavily to try to understand what makes you pick a bottle off the shelf. Once you've tried a bottle, try to remember whether you liked it or not – no mean feat when you're standing in front of a wine shelf. I take snaps and save them on my phone.

Glass

You can tell a lot about a wine by how it looks in the glass. You can check there's not something wrong with it, which is partly done using colour (see the Troubleshooting appendix for more on this). Swirling the glass also shows how much the wine coats the glass – the traces left are called legs or gothic arches, because of the shape made by the wine trickling down the glass. Aside from being pretty they are a good indicator of sweetness or alcohol – but not an indicator of quality.

The colour of a wine can be influenced by a number of things:

○ The colour and thickness of the grape skin. (The thicker the skin the stronger the colour.)
○ The age of the wine. (As wines get older they fade and tend to lose their vibrant colour.)
○ The amount of oak used. (Oak ageing tends to give white wine a deeper gold colour)

Whether you're drinking a £5 or £50 bottle of wine you can give it the best chance possible by presenting it in nice glasses, perhaps a carafe or *pichet* – and consider an ice bucket for chilled whites or sparklers. If you are trying to impress someone you can influence their opinion before they've even opened their mouth!

TOUCH

Touch is a bit more abstract, and for our purposes it's about the way the wine feels in your mouth. This differs dramatically from wine to wine, and can be influenced by a number of factors: alcohol, acidity, sweetness, tannin, grape and oak ageing.

Words to describe mouth feel

mean harsh meaty
Crunchy light round crisp
velvety
smooth oily creamy
heavy tingly luscious lively
delicate hollow prickly
supple grippy medium
tart rich simple fat fleshy
fine robust full-bodied
soft crisp rough sturdy
broad
big thin silky flat rustic
firm

Light wines

Light wine is produced in a simple way, not aged for long and
not aged in oak. This could be a red, white or rosé wine. In
your mouth it feels light, probably tastes dry and has a fresh
fruit taste. The flavour intensity isn't going to knock you off
your chair but that doesn't mean it's unpleasant. In
winemaking terms, not much has happened to this wine: no
barrel ageing, early-picked grapes, winemaking processes that
enhance the fruit quality and little else. Light wines are simple
in their structure and are happy to be chilled down so are
great refreshers (and this includes reds like Beaujolais or

Cabernet Franc). These wines are unfazed by being served without food but equally are a bit of a lifesaver when it comes to matching delicate food to wine. They are also great wines to have at a party or if you're planning to have a few glasses across the course of the evening: light wines are often (although not always) lighter in alcohol and therefore a bit easier on the head and body!

Examples of light wines
Muscat Sec, Pinot Grigio, Pinot Gris, Côtes de Provence, Beaujolais, Albariño, Tarrango, Cabernet Franc (Loire reds).

Medium wines
Medium wine has been on more of a journey than the lighter wines. It might not be bone dry, so it's got a tiny bit of sugar making the wine a bit swishier and more viscous. The sugar probably comes from grapes grown in sunnier climes, which have got just a bit riper and juicier. Medium wines are higher in tannins, which are in the skin and pips of the grapes and on their own taste green and bitter. You can normally detect the tannins by a slightly dry effect in your mouth, particularly around the gums. If they are done well the tannins allow the wine to stand up to a whole host of foods. Medium wine may also have spent some time in oak barrels, giving it a silkier texture, as if the edges have been rounded off and softened: this is particularly the case for tannic red wines. It can also give the impression of amplifying the wine and beefing it up a bit.

Examples of medium wines
Sauvignon Blanc, unoaked Chardonnay, Valpolicella, Fiano, Chianti, Pinot Noir (sometimes), Merlot, Carmenère.

Full-bodied wines

Full-bodied wines can knock you for six if you're not careful. Big in every way, these wines should come with a pair of safety boots and protective glasses. Generally these wines are high in alcohol, tannins and oak. They fill your mouth up, explode and leave you with something to chew over for a while. Much like the medium wines, they have often been through more processes – the grapes have spent more time sitting in the sun; the juice has fermented on the grape skins to get the tannins and colour; the wine has aged for months or years in barrels or bottles and the result is normally more complexity and more body. Because of this they are hard to drink on their own – it's like having a chargrilled steak on a plate with nothing else, or maybe just with a few iceberg lettuce leaves. It's too overpowering and your mouth doesn't know what to do with it. But matched with big food they can really hold their own. Those tannins are great with the textured steak and the smoky chargrill loves some oak. There was a time when big, full-bodied reds and whites were highly fashionable and every winemaker was trying to make their wine as punchy as possible, with lots of in-your-face flavours. Now it seems many winemakers are moving back to more restrained styles and making full-bodied wines that have a bit more subtlety and finesse.

Examples of full-bodied wines

New World reds like Australian Shiraz or Cabernet Sauvignon and Argentinean Malbec, White Burgundy and oaked Chardonnay, Rioja, Rhône Reds and Viognier.

Sparkling wine

When it comes to sparklers there are two things to consider: the wine itself and the bubbles. Both of these factors can be quite complex, as the wine has to be made differently in order for it to taste good when it's fizzy and, believe it or not, there

are various ways of getting bubbles into wine. The Fizz Line has a station for most of the main different sparklers and how and why they differ. As a taster here's my bubble scale showing the differences in sparkling wines.

- Vintage Champagne – a fine mousse, elegant bubbles and a rich mouth feel
- NV Champagne – lovely fine bubbles, crisp and smooth
- Traditional Method – crisper, with small bubbles, light and refreshing
- Cava – lively bubbles and a light mouth feel
- Prosecco – simple flavours, gentle bubbles
- Moscato – light bubbles, soft mouth feel

SMELL

Smell and taste are so inextricably linked that it's hard to separate them. A great way of proving this: try eating flavoured jelly beans with your nose held, test yourself to work out the flavours. They have the same texture, the same appearance and without smell are almost indistinguishable!

Smell is the most mysterious of our senses, and also the most evocative; it is more closely linked to memories than anything else and is more deeply linked into our psyche. Smell plays a massive role in the thousands of different kinds of wine that are out there and is therefore of paramount importance in helping you enjoy and discover new wines.

- Pour some wine into your glass and then swirl it round; you want to release all those smell molecules.
- Have a sniff – the more you stick your nose in and the more you inhale, the better the sensation will be.
- See if you can pick any smells out – common ones are fruit flavours (apple, melon, pineapple, lemon, cherries, blackcurrants), plants (herbs, mint, grass, flowers),

spices (vanilla, cinnamon, nutmeg, aniseed) or more
obscure scents (butter, wood, petrol, leather).

○ Try smelling two different wines side by side: with a
reference point you are more able to pick out the
differences.

Two things that can help or hinder how easy it is to smell are
temperature and your wine glass. Too cold and you suppress
the aromas; too hot and they fizzle off too quickly. Red wine
tends to need a bit more help to get it going, so warming it in
your glass by swirling it between your hands is more
important than with white wines.

TASTE

Our taste buds detect five different taste groups: sour, sweet,
bitter, salt and umami. Using these building blocks we build a
picture for our brain, which matches those building blocks to
the message it's receiving from the nose.

Take a sip of wine and, if you're feeling brave, swoosh it
round your mouth. In a good wine all the elements (acidity,
sweetness, tannin, alcohol) will be present but none of them
will overwhelm the others – you're looking for balance.

What you're looking for

Acidity – the backbone of a wine, it gives the wine a fresh
quality and without it you end up with a flat sensation in the
mouth. High acidity makes your mouth water, it feels
refreshing and keeps your palate clean. It is more noticeable
generally in white wine than red, because the tannins in red
wine are more obvious and almost mask the acidity. So when
you're comparing wines make a mental note of how much
your mouth has watered.

Sugar – while dry wines tend to taste clean and refreshing, sugar is a lot more obvious if you look for texture as well; you're looking for that gorgeous swishiness that feels like more than water. The sweetest wines in the world have an amazing level of acidity to cut through the sugar and prevent you from feeling like you're drinking golden syrup. Wines are often less sweet than we think because our brain confuses the aromas of sweet fruit with actual sweetness – look out for the fuller texture to work out how sweet a wine really is.

Tannin – this is a lot less present in our everyday life than sugar and acidity and so can be a bit more shocking on the mouth. Like the acidity, it provides structure, because without tannins you're back to alcoholic fruit juice. Tannins have an amazing way of drying your mouth and making it pucker. In a young, big wine from somewhere like Bordeaux you almost have to prise your mouth back open after a sip; in other wines the tannins slide down and feel smooth and creamy.

Alcohol – in a really good wine the alcohol is so well packaged in the flavours, acidity, tannins and sweetness that it can be imperceptible (which can be dangerous!). Sometimes you get a whiff of alcohol on the nose but normally if you can sense it in the mouth it tends to be a hotspot in the middle of your tongue – a bit like ginger or spiciness.

Prosecco ⊙

Cava ⊙

Traditional Method ⊙

Non Vintage Champagne ⊙

Vintage Champagne ⊙

Demi-sec / Semi-seco ⊙ ○

Pink Fizz Ⓢ

Red Fizz Ⓢ

Pink Champagne ⊙ ○

Ⓢ   style of wine

🍇   grape type

🌐   geographical region

⊙   official name for a wine

1. The Fizz Line

What introduction does a line called Fizz require? It's all about the bubbles here, and the diversity of styles, flavours, price and occasions you can drink them. Because bubbles are not just about the celebratory toast or glass on arrival at a party; they can also form a fundamental part of eating and drinking. So the Fizz Line takes you on a journey from frothy Moscato to everyday fizzes, and from affordably priced champagne-alikes to the top-end vintage stuff.

When to take the Fizz Line

As often as you can! Seriously – the range of bubbles available means there is one for every occasion and at prices to match. Try Moscato on its own or with a slice of cake; pink and red fizz at parties or with a curry, and Champagne for serious food matching. Or drink any of them in the bath – just because you can.

Stations on the Fizz Line

Prosecco, Demi-Sec / Semi-Seco, Pink Fizz, Red Fizz, Pink Champagne, Vintage Champagne, NV Champagne, Traditional Method, Cava.

Prosecco

This wine has become the sparkler of choice for many people, bridging the gap between top-end fizz and everyday drinking.

What you need to know

○ Prosecco is both a grape and an Italian appellation – a DOC (see glossary) which has recently formed to ensure better quality in the wines. It is made in a slightly different way from Champagne, which makes the bubbles bigger and less structured, and the flavour fruitier.

○ Prosecco comes in a variety of styles. Confusingly, the driest is Brut; the medium is Extra Dry, while the sweetest is called Dry. We mostly see Brut or Extra Dry in the UK.

○ Prosecco is a straightforward, aromatic style of sparkling wine. Classically you taste apples and pears with a floral hint. The purity of the flavours makes it very versatile and easy to drink.

○ It is less acidic than Champagne, which means it's good for parties where you might have a few glasses.

○ Look out for wines marked DOCG Conegliano-Valdobbiadene, which are the Prosecco Superiore and are guaranteed to be higher quality.

Eating with Prosecco

Because of its lower acidity, Prosecco isn't as well suited to food as Champagne is, so you're better off sticking to nibbles and lighter dishes. Avoid anything fried or spicy so as not to overwhelm the bubbles.

Head to Venice to wander the streets and soak up the ancient grandeur until your feet get too tired. After that, why not hop on a water taxi to get around. If you're prepared for the eye-watering prices, visit Harry's Bar, the home of the Bellini, and then head off into the night and off the tourist trail for some Venetian tapas and a glass or two of bubbles.

Demi-sec / Semi-seco ⊙

Demi-sec (France) or Semi-seco (Spain) is a semi-sweet, softer style of fizz, perfect for a little indulgence, drinking at parties or with cake.

What you need to know

○ Demi-sec or Semi-seco literally means 'half-dry' and refers to a style of sparkling wine with a bit of extra sweetness.

○ Demi-sec is the French term for this half-dry wine, and probably the one you're most likely to see. Semi-seco means the same in Spanish, and so is mostly seen on Cava labels. Just to complete the language lesson, in German you would say halbtrocken.

○ Most Champagne, Cava and Traditional Method wines are very dry with high acidity, which is great in a number of ways but is sometimes a bit much if you're drinking it over a long period of time, or if you're feeling a bit fragile. Demi-sec has just a bit of extra sweetness, which is added after the bubbles are formed. It's worth noting that, while almost all Champagne styles have a certain amount of sugar added (called the 'dosage') to take the edge off the high acidity, Demi-sec / Semi-seco has just a bit more. This extra sugar means you can actually taste the sweetness and the wine tends to feel a bit softer and richer in the mouth.

- Demi-sec / Semi-seco is great if you find normal champagne styles a bit too sharp, if you like drinking bubbles while eating cake, or if you're at Wimbledon and need something to wash down those strawberries . . .

Eating with Demi-sec / Semi-seco

This style of fizz works well as a drink on its own, particularly if you're not a fan of the high acidity of Champagne. However, the match made in heaven is a classic afternoon tea – and for the full effect, try to find a Demi-sec from England. It works perfectly as an aperitif, with the crustless sandwiches and especially with the scones.

Visiting Demi-sec / Semi-seco

These wines are made in the same way and place as their dry counterparts, so also have a look at the stations for Champagne, Cava and Traditional Method wines. One idea if you want to visit Demi-sec is to head to Paris and visit a patisserie full of those lovely smells of baking pastry and spun sugar, which is just what Demi-sec fizz smells like! And then there are all the macarons, madeleines and chocolates to try . . .

Pink Fizz

See the Easy Loop p. 74.

Red Fizz

See the Easy Loop p. 73.

Pink Champagne (S)

There is something extremely indulgent about Pink Champagne. It's not as readily available as Champagne – and neither is it just for girls! It is more full-bodied and a bit softer in the mouth than Champagne, and works well for many occasions.

What you need to know

○ Pink Champagne is unusual because, unlike most rosé wines, it is usually made by adding a tiny bit of red wine into a white blend, giving it a peachy, salmon-pink colour. Because of this, it maintains the crisp acidity of Champagne while intensifying the flavour and mouth feel, making it a fabulous foodie sparkler.

○ As with Champagne, house styles differ, as does the classification from Non-Vintage to Grand Cru. The Non-Vintages tend to be the freshest and lightest, while further up the scale, just like Champagne, you get a more intense, complex wine.

○ Unlike Champagne, however, Pink Champagne doesn't tend to age very well, so looking out for an old vintage won't necessarily mean you get a better wine.

Eating with Pink Champagne

Pink Champagne is extremely versatile when it comes to food: the extra body and flavour combine with the food-friendly acidity, making it great for tapas, buffets, cold meats and tomato dishes.

Visiting Pink Champagne

Épernay should be the next stop on your Champagne tour. It's dubbed the 'home of Champagne', and you'll see why when you wander along the impressive Avenue de Champagne, where many of the most famous brands have their homes. The Renaissance buildings, parks and leafy boulevards – not to mention the Champagne tastings – give a taste of the good life. And that's not all: underneath the streets lie 100km of cellars housing the Champagne that's not yet ready to be sold. Quite a thought!

Vintage Champagne (S)

Vintage Champagne doesn't fall into the everyday luxury category for most people. It's a different drink from NV Champagne and best saved for special moments.

What you need to know

○ Champagne producers (known as houses) don't make a 'vintage' champagne every year; as standard they blend the different crops together to make a Non-Vintage wine (as described in the previous section). However, in years where the producers consider the wine to be good enough, they 'declare' the vintage and make a Champagne using only that year's wine.

○ Vintage Champagnes are likely to be richer and more complex than NV Champagnes, due to the fact that they are aged longer on the yeasts in the bottle.

○ As Champagne is aged it goes from being very light and crisp to having more savoury flavours. It's often referred to as 'biscuity' and can smell a bit like baking bread.

○ At the pinnacle of Vintage Champagnes are the 'Cuvée Prestige' labels of the big Champagne houses, such as Louis Roederer's Cristal, Moët & Chandon's Dom Pérignon and Veuve Cliquot's La Grande Dame. These are the best of the best and you pay a lot of money for them.

○ The vintage really does make a difference to the style and quality of the Champagne. You can find lists of vintage years on the internet: look out for 1995 and 1996, which can be found on sale now and are considered to be among the very best.

Eating with Vintage Champagne

Vintage Champagne is an excellent match to food, particularly if you accentuate those yeasty flavours. But as each vintage differs, you should take your lead from the wine itself, which should give you some clues. Don't be afraid to match Vintage Champagne with dishes containing wild mushrooms, parmesan and, if you're lucky, truffles.

Visiting Vintage Champagne

If you're on a Champagne voyage (*see NV Champagne*), you can't miss out the town of Reims (pronounced *Ran-s*). This compact little town has pedestrian areas, bistros and, of course, Champagne shops where you can do mini tastings. It is also home to a stunning cathedral, which is well worth a wander, particularly for the blue stained-glass windows by Marc Chagall.

NV Champagne

The pop of a Champagne cork is enough to brighten even the darkest day. These are sophisticated bubbles from the Champagne region of France, suitable for hatches, matches and dispatches, as well as other notable occasions.

What you need to know

○ NV stands for Non-Vintage, which is the 'standard' level of Champagne. The producers blend together wines from different years to make the base wine, which is why Moët & Chandon or Veuve Cliquot yellow label always taste the same.

○ Most Champagne consists of Chardonnay, Pinot Noir and Pinot Meunier grapes (which you only find in Champagne), but the producer can decide what proportions, if any at all, of each they use. Pinot Noir and Pinot Meunier are red-skinned grapes with white flesh – the juice is extracted carefully to prevent the wine going pink.

○ Champagnes made with more Chardonnay are rounder and fuller-bodied, while more Pinot Noir gives the Champagne a more subtle, light flavour. Blanc de Blancs is pure Chardonnay and Blanc de Noir is pure Pinot Noir.

○ It's not all about the big names in this category: there are an increasing number of stockists selling Champagnes from lesser-known producers. These aren't always more expensive, but they often have more flavour and character.

Eating with Champagne

While it is a great stand-alone drink, Champagne is surprisingly good at being matched with food because of its acidity and body, particularly for slightly oily textures. This makes it the perfect wine with fish and chips – at any significant life events, whether they are in the new house, on the pier or just because you can't be bothered to cook!

Visiting Champagne

Champagne is a fabulous place to visit, and it's not too far from the UK, really. A morning Eurostar to Paris and then a train on to Épernay will get you there in a civilised manner. Of course, you might want to take the car so you can fill up your boot while visiting some of the big-name Champagne houses. Each has its own slant on the Champagne story, and although they can be a bit Disneyfied, they're worth a visit. You can always balance the spin by visiting some of the smaller producers. There are two main towns in the Champagne region – Épernay and Reims – which are covered in the following two entries.

Traditional Method Ⓢ

Although the term isn't very romantic, the 'traditional method' is the classic way of making Champagne and refers to a lengthy process that produces the finest bubbles and most intensely flavoured sparkling wines in the world.

What you need to know

○ Traditional-method wines are the 'champagne' of every country and tend to be elegant and refined fizzes.

○ The 'method' refers to the fizz-making stage of the process, where the base wine is made and bottled, and sugar and yeast are then added to each individual bottle to create a secondary fermentation which causes the bubbles. Because the bubbles are created in such a small space, they tend to be finer and more elegant than the bubbles found in other types of fizz.

○ Because the wine is in such close contact with the yeast, it tends to pick up a more complex flavour – a bit less fruity, with more of a savoury note. In young wines there's a hint of bakery about the wine; in older wines it's more like mushrooms.

○ Most traditional-method wines are made using the classic Champagne grapes of Chardonnay and Pinot Noir and therefore taste similar, although this isn't always the case.

○ Winemakers around the world use this method to make wines that can be as good as Champagne. Most English sparkling wine is made in this way, as well as the best of the Californian and Australian sparklers, and Crémant, which is the French term for traditional-method wines made outside the region of Champagne.

- The difference in all of these wines is often just the climate: as a rule the warmer/sunnier the area, the fruitier the grapes become, and this translates to a richer wine. The less sunny English climate produces sparkling wine that's crisper and drier than, say, Californian fizz, which tends to be rounder and creamier.
- It might not always be obvious from the label that the wine is made in the traditional method. Depending on the producer, traditional-method wines might also be referred to as *méthode traditionelle* or even just as having used traditional Champagne-making processes.

Eating with Traditional Method
The country of origin will dictate your food choice to a certain extent: English sparkling wine tends to be very light and delicate and has a hint of the hedgerow about it, so try it with asparagus, or very delicate fish dishes. Some of the New World wines are a bit rounder, less crisp, and seem to work extremely well on their own, but equally they can stand up to slightly richer starters, particularly with butter sauces.

Visiting Traditional Method
This has to be a visit to the south coast of England or Wales, where there are a growing number of vineyards, ranging from virtual smallholdings to relatively big sites. However, it's not like visiting Champagne, and many don't have visitor facilities. If you do have a favourite, get in touch in advance as many will give you a tour (and possibly a taster!) if you arrange to visit.

Cava

Spain's answer to Champagne, Cava is made using the same process, but because of the warmer climate and different combination of grapes used, it's a completely different glass of bubbly.

What you need to know

○ Cava is a bright, fruity sparkler with crisp acidity and a lively fizz.

○ Cava can be made using traditional Champagne grapes as well as local Spanish ones. The resulting Cava will taste different depending on the blend used. Local grape varieties have a distinctive, often earthy flavour, which is not to everyone's taste.

○ Like Champagne, Cava can differ enormously between extremely dry (*brut nature*) and sweet (*dulce*), making it really versatile, and there's rosé on top of that.

○ Cava has a bit of a tarnished reputation for being cheap and not so nice, but that's only really at the bargain-basement end of the budget. If you spend the same on Cava as you would on Prosecco or some of the New World fizzes, you will get fantastic value for money.

○ Cava has a similar bubble structure to Champagne – small, firm bubbles that won't go flat if you add other substances to them – so you can use Cava instead of Champagne in recipes for Champagne cocktails. It makes a great alternative and won't break the bank.

Eating with Cava

The key to a food-friendly fizz is acidity, and Cava has this in spades. In Barcelona you would have a glass with your tapas and let the acidity clear your palate. At home, pair it with cold meats and cheeses or seafood such as tempura prawns. Steer clear of too much chilli, which does not complement the acidity and the bubbles.

Visiting Cava

Catalonia is Cava country (although it does come from other areas of Spain too) so head to Barcelona and explore the bars and try some tapas. The old town is a maze of lanes packed with shops, bars and restaurants, and just a couple of turns away from touristy Las Ramblas will take you off the beaten track. It's worth making an effort to hunt out some of the smaller places, where the atmosphere is completely different, full of locals enjoying a glass of Cava and a plate of tapas. Once you're off the tourist trail, it's excellent value too.

Vinho Verde ⊙

Grüner Veltliner 🍇

Semillon 🍇

Sauvignon Blanc 🍇

Rueda ⊙

Chenin Blanc 🍇

Gavi ⊙

White Rioja ⊙

Fiano 🍇

Chardonnay 🍇

White Burgundy 🌐

 S   style of wine

🍇   grape type

🌐   geographical region

⊙   official name for a wine

2. The White Central Line

The White Central Line is the backbone of white wines on the WineTubeMap, as it contains both Sauvignon Blanc and Chardonnay, two of the world's most popular white wines. The wines on this line range from very light and refreshing to full-bodied and creamy, but they all have an inherent fruitiness, whether it's citrus or tropical.

When to take the White Central Line
One of the key things about this line is its versatility: most of the wines lend themselves to food matching, although few are so big and beefy that you can't just settle down and have a glass on its own. Take this line for dinner parties and restaurant wine lists, and when you need a classic wine to deliver the goods.

Stations on the White Central Line
Vinho Verde, Grüner Veltliner, Semillon, Sauvignon Blanc, Rueda, Chenin Blanc, Gavi, White Rioja, Fiano, Chardonnay, White Burgundy.

Vinho Verde

This unusual white wine is very light, almost green in colour. Vinho Verde is enjoying a revival at the moment due to some improvements in the winemaking process: many wineries have updated their equipment in order to keep the wines cooler in the winery, which means they can get the kind of fresher, crisper, fruitier-tasting wine that most people are looking for.

What you need to know

O Vinho Verde is a Portuguese style of wine meaning 'green wine' or 'young wine'.

O It is one of the lightest wines on the WineTubeMap, with a delicate flavour and dry finish. The wine is made with local grapes, including Alvarhino (known as Albariño in Spain).

O Vinho Verde was traditionally lower in alcohol and had a slight spritz (also known as *petillance*), although this is less common now. The new wave of winemakers are making slightly more full-bodied and aromatic styles.

O Vinho Verde is often thought of as a 'holiday drink', reminiscent of sunny days in Portugal where it makes the perfect aperitif after a hard day's relaxing. Back at home you might need to create a sunshine feeling in your kitchen!

O It is traditionally a young wine, so it's not to be stored or saved – and check that the vintage is current. It might be last year but shouldn't be any older.

Eating with Vinho Verde

Stay light and fresh here – the appeal of Vinho Verde is its freshness and delicacy, so it works well with simple, light dishes. Try pairing it with salads, seafood, fresh peas or asparagus.

Visiting Vinho Verde

Vinho Verde is made just north of Porto, the home of Port, in the northernmost tip of Portugal. The area is vibrant and green due to the climate (it's a wet part of the country) and the landscape ranges from lush valleys and mountains to a sandy coastline. The area is famous for its local markets and traditional fiestas, so plan your trip around one of these to get a real taste of local life.

Grüner Veltliner

This 'on-trend' crisp white wine comes from Austria. Whereas only five years ago you would not have found Grüner Veltliner on shop shelves anywhere in the UK, now no retailer would be seen without it, and rightly so.

What you need to know

- Grüner Veltliner is a grape found in Austria and across eastern Europe. New Zealand has recently hopped aboard the bandwagon, with some producers planting Grüner Veltliner vines.
- The wines you find in the UK are a lovely blend of crunchy apple crispness, white peaches and a mild pepperiness, making them delicate and elegant. They're great with food but also a super fridge standby.

- For the best wines look for the name Wachau on the label: this region is Austria's best growing area and produces a distinctive style.
- The Austrians also make a more serious Grüner Veltliner wine which is aged, and over time it becomes richer and more spicy. It's unusual to find the older wines in the UK – and they would be a bit pricier – but if you do find one, snap it up!

Eating with Grüner Veltliner

This wine is very versatile, and the potential for food matching ranges from tempura prawns with chilli sauce to a Sunday roast chicken or roast pork. Steer clear of anything too spicy, too earthy or too meaty.

Visiting Grüner Veltliner

Vienna is an unusual city because of the vineyards within its confines, so you can book a city break and indulge in some wine tasting while you're there. Only an hour from Vienna, the Wachau region is an improbable landscape for winemaking, with steep and rocky slopes covered in tiny vineyards flanking the Danube. Austria is known for its Heurigen, a kind of wine tavern, where wineries open their doors to share the new vintage with visitors. The food is simple and the company convivial. It's a good idea to get some local knowledge about the best ones to visit, as they aren't all open all of the time and some are more authentic than others.

Semillon

A less well-known white grape that features in French classics and shines in Australia.

What you need to know
- Semillon plays a number of different roles, depending on where you are in the world.
- Unoaked and young, it is a lively and vibrant, lemon sherbet mouthful – best sampled from the Hunter Valley in Australia.
- When aged, it becomes richer and oilier, a real swish-in-your-mouth kind of wine where that citrus flavour is caramelised. Hunter Valley wines age well, as do wines from Barossa. These are typically aged in oak, which, combined with a hotter climate, gives the wine even more opulence.
- Blended with Sauvignon Blanc, it is the secret weapon in White Bordeaux (or Bordeaux Blanc) and the iconic sweet wine Sauternes. This blend is also very successful in Australia's Margaret River region. The two grapes combine to create a great balancing point between flavour and texture.

Eating with Semillon
Semillon is a great match for 'fusion' cooking, where light, fresh ingredients meet Asian flavours like lemongrass, chilli, ginger and coriander. The lighter wines are superb with seafood and fish dishes while the bigger wines are good with creamy sauces and smoky flavours.

Visiting Semillon
The Hunter Valley is only three hours north of Sydney, so it's an easy trip to tag on while in New South Wales. There are so many wineries and foodie places to visit that you will need an itinerary of breakfast, lunch and dinner spots! Be sure to look out for local events and entertainment as there is always something going on.

Sauvignon Blanc

One of the world's most popular and ubiquitous white grapes, Sauvignon Blanc goes by many names depending on where you are in the world. For many it is the go-to wine for any occasion.

What you need to know
- The word most associated with Sauvignon Blanc is 'cool'. Not only because no one ever turns up their nose if you order a glass of Sauvignon, but also because it grows best in cool regions, and because you should drink it very cool!
- Sauvignon is identifiable by its racy acidity, pale colour and zesty, grassy and gooseberry flavours. It does differ dramatically depending on where it's grown, but it maintains these main attributes across the board.
- Don't bother laying it down. Sauvignon Blanc is nearly always best drunk sooner rather than later, so look out for this year's or last year's vintage.
- This also means that there are very few reasons to store Sauvignon Blanc in anything but a screwcap to keep it fresh.

Homes of Sauvignon Blanc

FRANCE

Classically found in Sancerre and Pouilly-Fumé (regions facing each other on the River Loire), these wines have citrus notes with a highly characteristic gooseberry flavour and a flinty smokiness. Less tropical and grassy than New World styles, these are fantastic wines with shellfish and smoked salmon. Sauvignon Blanc is widely grown in the rest of the Loire Valley under the banner of Touraine Sauvignon. While the quality can vary, these offer a good budget alternative to a Sancerre.

NEW ZEALAND

Now the go-to country for Sauvignon Blanc, New Zealand has its own distinctive style when it comes to this white wine. It is intensely green in flavour with grassy, gooseberry and asparagus flavours. The Marlborough region has been the benchmark until now, making its name with the famous Cloudy Bay winery in the 1990s. Unfortunately this popularity has led to a degree of mass production and these days some wines that are less than stunning have the name Marlborough on the label. Recently some interesting wines have been coming out of the Waipara and Hawke's Bay areas. Look for the name of a producer rather than a brand name to help pick out the good wines.

CHILE

For a while now, Chilean Sauvignon Blanc has been on every wine list and shop shelf. And there's a reason for this: Chile makes good mid-price wines that are fruity, well balanced and easy drinking. More tropical than either French or New Zealand styles, with rounder, creamier palates, Chilean Sauvignon Blancs have the right balance to handle more complex foods and flavours.

AUSTRALIA

Definitely not what Australia is known for, but Australian Sauvignon Blanc, when it's done well, is really exciting. It has to come from a cool region like Adelaide Hills or Margaret River, and these wines have a more limey, tropical flavour, great for the big outdoors and chilling on a deckchair in the sun. They also make a great match for Thai food.

Eating with Sauvignon Blanc

A great wine to pair with starters, Sauvignon Blanc is a match made in heaven with goat's cheese, asparagus, sushi and shellfish, which can all be a bit awkward to match otherwise. The more restrained styles of Sauvignon Blanc from France and Chile are more versatile than the in-your-face New Zealand wines, which can overpower some foods.

Visiting Sauvignon Blanc

This is a toss-up between Sancerre and Marlborough. If you're off to New Zealand, be sure to enjoy a vineyard tour on a hired bike – liberating, fun, picturesque and bountiful all at once. Life in New Zealand is geared towards adventure, so go kayaking around the waterways of the Sounds (fjords) and earn your dinner!

If you're in France you can visit Sancerre and Pouilly-Fumé as part of a pilgrimage to the home of Sauvignon Blanc. The region is about two hours south of Paris. Make sure you stop off in Chavignol for some of their famous goat's cheese (paired with Sancerre, *bien sûr*!).

Rueda

This less well-known Spanish region produces white wines with a similar character to Sauvignon Blanc. Sometimes you get tired of one wine and you want to try something a bit different. Well, that's where Rueda comes in.

What you need to know

- Rueda is a Spanish denomination from central Spain, north-west of Madrid, and although it is an old region there has been a recent move to this younger, fresher style of white wine.
- The main grape in the blend is almost always Verdejo, combined either with local grapes or Sauvignon Blanc (although sometimes you get pure Verdejo or pure Sauvignon Blanc).
- Rueda has the crisp, citrus flavours people love about Sauvignon Blanc but it's a more subtle wine. Some winemakers age their wines in oak – not for the flavour so much as the texture.

Eating with Rueda

Rueda is extremely easy to pair with food, and equally easy to drink on its own. Don't sweat too much about complex foods; instead focus on enjoying yourself. Goat's cheese, tabbouleh and calamari are all excellent matches.

Visiting Rueda

The Rueda area is in the Castilla y Leon region of Spain, easily accessed in under an hour by high-speed train from Madrid. It is a charming area where tradition meets the modern world in every aspect. High-tech architectural wineries are springing up alongside traditional ones and Roman ruins provide the backdrop to modern Spanish cuisine.

Chenin Blanc

This grown-up grape doesn't always get the credit it deserves. It makes sophisticated and subtle wines in both France and South Africa, but unfortunately it makes some unmemorable wines too.

What you need to know

○ Chenin Blanc is a jack of all trades, originating from the Loire Valley in France. It can be made into every style of white wine, from cutting dry wines through medium-bodied and oak-aged varieties into Champagne-style sparklers and world-class sweeties.

○ It is the base grape in Vouvray and many of the Crémant de Loire sparklers.

○ The grape itself can be very neutral and acidic but in the right hands it can be made into world-class wines, and the acidity means it can age well too.

○ Chenin Blanc has a slightly unusual flavour profile of peaches and pears with honeysuckle and lots of honey in the richer wines. In lesser wines you tend to get high acidity and a flavour like pear drops.

○ It has also been adopted as a South African mainstay, where the barrel-aged Chenin Blancs can be very classy.

Eating with Chenin Blanc

This is potentially the most versatile white wine on the WineTubeMap – you can match it with almost anything. The high acidity cuts through oil and fat easily, making it a great partner for fish and chips. The richer styles have a hint of umami and work wonders with Japanese food and roasted or caramelised flavours. It is also a great autumnal wine, capable of standing up to more robust flavours and textures.

Visiting Chenin Blanc

You might call Vouvray, in the Loire Valley, the home of Chenin Blanc, where they make everything from bone-dry sparklers to lush sweeties. A visit there could be added on to a trip to Sancerre, Pouilly-Fumé or Chinon (*see Sauvignon Blanc* and *Cabernet Franc*) to make a week-long holiday of touring wine routes, stopping off at small, traditional producers and indulging in the local cheeses and wines. Or perhaps head to Stellenbosch in South Africa for a completely different Chenin Blanc experience. Stay in a plush hotel in a winery and immerse yourself in the experience.

Gavi ◉

An Italian restaurant wine list stalwart which could make its way on to your wine rack at home.

What you need to know

○ Gavi is an appellation (DOCG) from northern Italy. Popular in the 1960s and '70s, it's rather fallen out of favour in recent years, but at its best it can be a really great wine.

○ The grape is called Cortese, which you rarely see anywhere else.

○ Gavi isn't a blockbuster wine; it's light, fresh and lemony with great acidity. With more flavour and often more structure, it offers a great alternative to Pinot Grigio.

○ Quality can be a variable with Gavi, and there is little on the label to help you out: it's best to go to trusted sources and get recommendations. You sometimes see 'Gavi di Gavi' on the label, but this doesn't guarantee any specific quality or style.

Eating with Gavi

Gavi is good with light, simple dishes like lemon sole, relatively plain roast chicken or just some nibbles. It is an easy crowd pleaser and a nice drop to keep in the fridge if you just fancy a glass on its own.

Visiting Gavi

The traditional village of Gavi is on the cusp of the Piedmont and Genovese regions of northern Italy, and it's a great place to explore Italian cooking. The landscape is rural, with ruined hilltop fortresses presiding over small farms and villages. Hire a car and explore at your leisure.

White Rioja

White Rioja (or Rioja Blanco) has suffered from bad press and inconsistent quality over the years, but there are some gems to be found if you know what to look for. This controversial and often unpopular wine has a hidden soul – if you can find it!

What you need to know

○ Hailing from the Rioja region, much more famous for its red wines, these whites are tiny in comparison but are enjoying a mini revolution.

○ White Rioja falls into three categories – the traditional, the new and the ones with a foot in both camps.

○ The traditional is not for the faint-hearted: it is heavily oaked and isn't readily available. Their labels often include 'Reserva' or 'Gran Reserva' because of the oak ageing – these are the hardest White Riojas to get on with and the least popular. The great examples can be intensely nutty and a delicious surprise.

○ The new whites are crisp, dry and refreshing, made to reflect the popularity of zesty Sauvignon Blanc. White Riojas made with 100% Viura (also known as Macabeo) grapes tend to be the most balanced, although wineries are now allowed to include international grape varieties so you will see Sauvignon Blanc in some. It will often be marked 'joven' (young) because it hasn't been oak-aged.

○ The wines with a foot in both camps are a newer, fresher style of barrel-fermented White Rioja, which is rich and tropical with a gentle spiciness. It is more full-bodied than the new 'joven' style, but much fruitier than the old style. The key is that the wine is actually made in a barrel for texture rather than flavour, so you get a lovely creamy style but no overwhelming whack of oak.

Eating with White Rioja

You can be pretty flexible with food matching. The new-style unoaked wines are great with cold meats, green salads and fresh tomatoes. The barrel-fermented wines have a bit more texture, so pair them with fleshy fish in creamy sauces or a Spanish dish such as tortilla. The old style are a bit trickier, but a good one has a savoury edge, perfect for a richer, more complex dinner.

Visiting White Rioja

This would be much the same as a visit to Red Rioja! The capital Logroño is a gastronomic destination in its own right, and is a lot more authentic than trendy-but-touristy San Sebastian. In the old town you will find a bustling tapas scene where you can hop from bar to bar, eating a few tapas at each and washing it down with a glass or two. Heaven!

Fiano

A little-known gem from Italy. Many people assume that Italian whites are all like Pinot Grigio, which is why Fiano and some of the other southern Italian wines are such a delightful surprise.

What you need to know
- Fiano is a white grape grown in the south of Italy and Sicily.
- A latecomer to the UK, recent improvements to the winemaking have suddenly brought it to popularity and on to restaurant wine lists.
- Unlike many white wines, it's more than just fruity: it has a savoury note with a nutty spiciness and ripe texture as well as a very ripe apple flavour.
- There is also the more premium-quality Fiano di Avellino DOCG appellation, which is the grape grown in a specific area to more controlled standards. These wines can be double the price, but are worth it for a special occasion.
- There is an extension to this line of other similar grapes from the Campania region in southern Italy – Falanghina and Greco di Tufo are just two others to try.

Eating with Fiano
Because of its fuller body and structure, this is a great wine to match with some bolder Italian dishes. Try it with smoky carbonara sauce, grilled oily fish or hearty filled pasta.

Visiting Fiano

The south of Italy and Sicily are relatively untouched by tourism, which makes them attractive places to visit, especially in spring and autumn when the weather is slightly cooler. Visit the numerous small towns and join in the custom of the '*passeggiata*' – taking a stroll through the streets in early evening, stopping for an aperitif or ice cream and enjoying a spot of people watching.

Chardonnay

The most versatile and best-known white grape which, despite its versatility, has suffered a bit of an identity crisis in recent years.

What you need to know

○ Chardonnay is grown almost everywhere that wine is made in the world, including the UK! It makes up some of the world's greatest wines and some of the most basic ones when used as part of a blend.

○ The grape is quite neutral in flavour and character so takes its style from the climate, vineyards and winemaker's process. But it isn't bland: the potential for Chardonnays range from light and crisp to rich and buttery.

○ The trend towards 'Anything but Chardonnay' was the result of a decade of very fruity, heavily oaked Chardonnays coming out of Australia. To begin with they were popular for their easy-drinking style but soon there were many 'me too' brands of average quality which put people off. But saying you don't like Chardonnay is a bit like saying you don't like chicken – it can be prepared and presented in so many ways that there are bound to be some styles you like better than others.

- As a rule, unoaked Chardonnay is crisp and citrussy, becoming more tropical as it goes into warmer climates. Oaked Chardonnay tends to be more full-bodied, with a distinctive buttery or even butterscotch flavour.
- Chardonnay is a key ingredient in Champagne and sparkling wines. It's also the grape used to make Chablis.

Eating with Chardonnay
Chardonnay has quite a lot of body, even unoaked, so pair it with dishes with texture and body. Steer clear of aromatic spices and chillies as they will just exacerbate the acidity and alcohol. The fuller-bodied Chardonnays can handle very complex savoury dishes – just pay a bit of attention to where the oak comes from. American oak is sweeter and doesn't match with savoury food quite so well.

Visiting Chardonnay
Why not make your Chardonnay pilgrimage in California? Touristy and pricey Napa Valley can be a bit full-on, so try a visit to the laidback Russian River area. The tiny town of Healdsberg in Sonoma Valley is a microcosm of cool that you can use as a base to visit the region's wineries. The wine region is only a couple of hours' drive from San Francisco, so you can combine it with a visit to this fabulous American city.

Styles of Chardonnay

BRANDS AND BLENDS
You can find some fabulous blends made with Chardonnay. However, when you see Chardonnay blended with Semillon or Sauvignon at around the £5 mark you are getting the benefit of its versatility and the popularity of the name rather than any real winemaking technique. It doesn't generally do the grape justice.

CRISP AND CITRUSSY
When Chardonnay is grown in cooler climates and is produced without using any oak, you get a crisp, refreshing wine bursting with fresh fruit flavours of apple, lemon and a hint of peach. You find it in Chablis, cool-climate Australian regions, parts of South America and Montana in the US.

MEDIUM-BODIED
These wines are silky, with more tropical fruit flavours like peach and pineapple, and if there is any oak it is subtle and light. Often the wine has spent some time with oak and it may have been through malolactic fermentation (converting the sharp acids to creamier ones). Chile and Argentina are particularly good at medium-bodied wines.

BIG, FAT CHARDONNAY
These wines have gone through the malolactic fermentation process to produce a buttery or even butterscotch flavour, often with a sweet vanilla edge or a smoky nature. These wines come from Australia, famous for those sweet vanilla and white chocolate notes, Chile and California for some of the smoky wines, and France for the more subtle buttery effect.

White Burgundy

This is a classic white wine, perhaps less popular now than in its heyday. It has a bit of snob factor, but get past that and there is a whole new world to discover.

What you need to know

- Part of the backbone of France, the Burgundy region runs from north to south, along the Saône River.
- Burgundy is split into numerous highly fragmented appellations, many of which we know almost like a brand. Some areas command sky-high prices while their neighbours sell for a fraction of the price – it's all about the name.
- The wines are almost all made with Chardonnay grapes but they differ due to climate, vineyard position and winemaking techniques.
- Classification means that within each appellation you can go up from generic AOC villages to premier cru, with grand cru at the top end (and at this point vintage becomes important).
- Chablis is one of the most famous wines, crisp and peachy with a classic note of gun flint. Many people don't realise it is Chardonnay!
- Pouilly-Fuissé (not to be confused with Pouilly-Fumé) is medium-bodied, crisp and fresh. At the other end of the scale, Meursault and Chassagne-Montrachet are rich and full, with a buttery and creamy texture. If your budget doesn't stretch that far, try the lesser-known appellations of Rully, Saint-Véran and Saint-Aubin, which offer better value for money.

Eating with White Burgundy

White Burgundy is refined, elegant and subtle in comparison to some other Chardonnays, which means you need food with a similar nature. Classic cooking seems to match it better, so that no single flavour dominates and each element, including the wine, allows the others to shine. I would suggest trying a classic roast chicken, seared scallops with a butter sauce or a mushroom risotto.

Visiting White Burgundy

Each appellation in White Burgundy has its own town or village, and they all differ slightly depending on the fortunes of the wine. Some are blink-and-you-miss-them villages, while others are bustling towns. All will have a little restaurant somewhere serving a very satisfactory *plat du jour* and carafe of the local wine. Just remember that in these towns, timing is crucial: it's often hard to find anywhere serving food after 2pm and even harder to find a restaurant open on a Sunday or Monday.

○ Muscat 🍇

○ Gewürztraminer 🍇

○ Viognier 🍇

○ Riesling 🍇

○ Albariño 🍇

○ Sauvignon Blanc 🍇

○ Pinot Gris 🍇

○ Pinot Grigio 🍇

S style of wine

🍇 grape type

🌐 geographical region

○ official name for a wine

3. The Aromatic Line

The Aromatic Line includes a mixture of old friends and new favourites, all sharing a slightly more flighty and exotic style. It encompasses a section of wines that range from sweet to dry, but all with a more perfumed, fragrant character than other white wines. They are deliciously moreish and the semblance of sweetness that you get from the aromatic nature can be very pleasing. These wines are often refreshing and food-friendly, which makes them versatile crowd pleasers.

When to take the Aromatic Line

This line moves from the lightest of light Pinot Grigio up to the heady Gewürztraminer and Muscat, so there isn't a one-size-fits-all aspect to these wines. The wines at the lighter end are great on their own, but as you go further along the line they can be a bit overpowering and need some food to accompany them. The slightly sweeter and more full-bodied nature of the wines at the top end of the line makes them great matches for aromatic foods. The balance of sweetness and acidity can complement chilli, lemongrass and ginger as well as being a surprisingly good match for cheese. These are wines to really impress your friends with.

Stations on the Aromatic Line

Pinot Grigio, Pinot Gris, Sauvignon Blanc, Albariño, Riesling, Viognier, Gewürztraminer, Muscat.

Pinot Grigio

The white wine that seems to be just about everywhere!

What you need to know

○ This is actually the same grape as Pinot Gris, but Pinot Grigio is the Italian name and tends to denote a light, crisp and easy-going style.

○ At its best it can be fruity and refreshing, but you need to pay more to get some real flavour. Cheap Pinot Grigio is often criticised for its neutral or bland flavours and high acidity. Because of this it is often served extremely chilled!

○ The richer Pinot Grigios tend to come from the Friuli region of Italy. If you want to make sure you're buying good quality, look for the DOCG on the official label on the bottle top. It means the wine has had to pass certain criteria to be classified.

Eating with Pinot Grigio

Commercial styles of Pinot Grigio are probably best served on their own or with snacks and crisps: they don't have the body or flavour profile to match up to many dishes. The richer, more fragrant styles are still very delicate, so steer clear of anything too spicy or pungent. Instead drink Pinot Grigio with spring flavours, crunchy salads and fish baked *en papillote*.

Visiting Pinot Grigio

Head to northern Italy for a blend of food and culture. The Friuli-Venezia Giulia region is a diverse area ranging from the Alps to the sea. There is plenty to explore and discover, from churches and frescoes to hill towns and beaches – not to mention cheese! The region has a strong Austro-Hungarian influence, so don't expect to find much pasta on the menu.

Pinot Gris

Pinot Gris is the French name for Pinot Grigio. The French wine is richer and riper than the Italian Pinot Grigio and these days Pinot Gris refers to this style, regardless of where the grapes are grown.

What you need to know

○ Pinot Gris is a much overlooked wine. For a long time it wasn't easily available in the UK, but you see it on shop shelves more often these days.

○ Although traditionally from Alsace, Germany and eastern Europe, you can also find Pinot Gris from Oregon in the north-west US, New Zealand, Australia and Tasmania.

○ Pinot Gris is a delicate, fresh wine, often floral with melon flavours and a smokiness on the finish. The New World wines, particularly from New Zealand, are drier, crisper and fresher.

○ The grapes are darker-skinned, resulting in wine that's almost pink in colour and a bit of a surprise if you're not expecting it!

Eating with Pinot Gris

Pinot Gris is a great friend of food, particularly dishes with a hint of spice (as are many of the wines on the Aromatic Line). It goes really well with mild curry sauces made with ground almonds, and Thai dishes such as spicy fish cakes. Pinot Gris is incredibly versatile and works well with many dishes, from pâté (a traditional Alsace match) to sushi.

 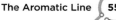

Like Gewürztraminer, Pinot Gris has a home in Alsace. Hire a gîte in a village, ideally with a pool, go shopping in the local town for a selection of deli goodies and have a poolside picnic. Pinot Gris is a classy grape, so dress for dinner.

Sauvignon Blanc ⊛

See the White Central Line p. 38.

Albariño ⊛

As stylish as the Spanish women trotting up Barcelona's Las Ramblas, this grape is a relative newcomer to our shelves but it is becoming increasingly popular in the UK.

What you need to know

○ Albariño is part of a Spanish revolution of interesting, easy-drinking wines. It's a great stepping stone between the crispness of Sauvignon Blanc and the ripe fruitiness of Viognier.

○ The wines we see in the UK are generally young and fresh, so you get a lovely peachy flavour with a dry finish and crisp bite. You do occasionally see an oak-aged or older wine, which will have a rounder texture and more honeyed flavour.

○ Albariño is not the cheapest wine as it's in limited production (although this is growing), but you do get great value for money as you rarely find a bad one.

- Albariño has paved the way for a number of other similar Spanish grapes and wine which are now appearing on our shelves: Godello, Treixadura (Tray-shay-dure-a) and Txakoli (Shack-oh-lee).

Eating with Albariño

This is definitely a wine to be enjoyed on its own at the end of a hard day, or on a summer afternoon in the garden. It's a versatile wine with food, so you can be bold and pair it with anything that isn't too heavy and meaty. Shellfish dishes are a definite yes, as are tapas plates and anything with fresh, crunchy vegetables. Steer clear of red meats and anything too creamy.

Visiting Albariño

Although you do occasionally see Albariño from California and Australia, its home is Galicia in the north-west of Spain. Despite its reputation for being the rainiest region of Spain, the summers are warm and sunny and the wine-growing Rías Baixas area is full of quiet, sandy beaches. The seafood is seriously good too, so pack your bucket and spade and discover a new part of Spain.

Riesling

A delicious chameleon, often thought of as a sweet wine but full of zesty, zingy flavours. It is pronounced Ree-zling, not Rye-sling.

What you need to know

- Forget the 1970s and the flabby, sweet wines that used to be sold in the UK: Riesling today is a world apart from those. Now produced around the world, the range of styles of Riesling means there's one out there for everyone. German and Alsace Rieslings are the absolute classics, varying from dry (*trocken*) to ultra sweet (*trockenbeerenauslese* – easier to say than you think).

O Chile, New Zealand and Australia produce drier, fresher styles. If you don't like the sweetness of some German Rieslings, look out for examples from Clare Valley in Australia, or New Zealand Rieslings, which are closer to Sauvignon Blanc in style.

O Wherever it comes from, Riesling is unique for its racy acidity, which offsets the sweetness and keeps the wine tasting fresh and zingy. This blend of sweetness and acidity is combined with a dollop of aromatic fruitiness, ranging from honeysuckle and blossom to crunchy apples or tropical favours like caramelised limes.

O Riesling is often significantly lower in alcohol than other grapes, especially the German wines.

O You can often notice something that smells a bit like petrol in older German Riesling and a lot of New World styles. It's considered a good thing but it does take a bit of getting used to. If you smell it you can impress people, as it's very specific to this grape.

Eating with Riesling

Riesling is an excellent food wine. The sweetness is great with chillies and the acidity and body mean it is a supreme match for Thai food – try zingier wines with salads and sweeter wines with Thai red curry. The lower alcohol is especially helpful with hot, spicy dishes as alcohol amplifies the heat. Riesling is also fantastic with pork dishes, particularly roast joints or pork belly. Think of it as the equivalent of apple sauce.

Visiting Riesling

Head to Mosel and the Rhine Valley where you can cycle, hike or take a boat trip to admire the romantic scenery. The hills are covered with tiny vineyards in places so steep it's hard to imagine how anyone gets up there. Go on a winery tour: it's a cliché but you'll get some stunning wines that never make it to the UK

Viognier

Possibly one of the grapes that people have the most trouble pronouncing, Viognier (Vee-on-yay) offers an unusual alternative to Sauvignon Blanc and Chardonnay. It has more perfume than either of those classic grapes, with a peachy flavour and a creamy texture.

What you need to know

○ Originally having made its name in the northern Rhône in France, this grape is now a worldwide winner. Look out for it in the south of France, South America and Australia.

○ Viognier is all about peaches and cream: whether you've picked a lighter version or a full-on luscious style, you can't miss the unmistakable flavours and texture.

○ Despite its very distinct style, Viognier seems to be a great converter – red lovers enjoy the bigger, rounder body; sweetie lovers like the ripeness and yet it is still a dry white wine.

○ You will often find Viognier in a blend where winemakers want to add a bit of oomph but don't want the full-on flavour – some red wines even have a drop of Viognier to lift them.

- If you want to blow the budget, indulge in some Condrieu – a French region where the wine is exclusively Viognier. It's expensive, but oh so worth it!

Eating with Viognier

Viognier has an interesting mix of flavour and body, which makes it a good white wine for matching with more robust meals. It can work well with Chinese dishes and it matches beautifully the sweetness of pumpkin, or fish and poultry dishes with caramelised or fruity flavours.

Visiting Viognier

Viognier can be found in many countries these days – take your pick from the south of France, coastal Chile or South Australia. If you were being traditional you would head to Condrieu but, despite its spectacular wines, it isn't necessarily the most tourist-friendly place. It might be worth heading to the Languedoc instead (*see the Red Central Line*).

Gewürztraminer

Exotic and spicy, Gewürztraminer can be a bit intimidating but sometimes it's worth a venture into the unknown!

What you need to know

- First things first, it is pronounced Ge-vürtz-trameen-er, although it is often shortened to the more manageable Ge-vurtz.
- Traditionally found in the Alsace region of France and parts of Germany, we are now seeing an increase of dry styles from New Zealand and Chile.

- Gewürztraminer has an unusual flavour, with a heady combination of exotic flavours like lychees, rose and Turkish delight. These flavours are quite divisive and it tends to be the kind of wine you either love or hate.
- Gewürztraminer also comes in a dessert wine, called Vendange Tardive.

Eating with Gewürztraminer

The unique flavours of Gewürztraminer lend themselves well to Indian and Thai food, as the sweetness of the wine offsets heat from chillies (up to a point). In addition, the wine's texture is great with coconut sauces and the aromatics work well with lemongrass and curry leaves. However, it's also surprisingly good with cheese, especially slightly smelly ones!

Visiting Gewürztraminer

Alsace is the spiritual home of Gewürztraminer. A visit to the region's picture-book towns for some hill-walking followed by hearty pork dishes and plentiful carbs makes a wonderful break – just don't expect to lose weight! You'll find far more interesting wines in Alsace than you do in the UK, so go on a wine-tasting tour – or if possible drive over and fill up your boot!

Muscat

See the Easy Loop p. 64.

Beaujolais ⊙

New World Rosé Ⓢ

Red Fizz Ⓢ

Pink Fizz Ⓢ

White Zinfandel 🍇

Grenache/ Garnacha Rosé 🍇

Prosecco ⊙

Côtes de Provence ⊙

Moscato Ⓢ

Muscat 🍇

4. The Easy Loop

The Easy Loop delivers exactly what it promises. It is relaxed and laidback, perfect for days when you don't know what to drink or you're pleasing a crowd. If you were Goldilocks, these would be the perfect wines for you: they're not too sharp, nor too tannic, nor too sweet or dry.

When to take the Easy Loop

These wines are great for parties, picnics and when you've just walked in the door and fancy a glass of something easy-going. They aren't big food wines, but there are quite a lot of stations on the Easy Loop that go well with chocolate and cakes as well as savoury nibbles. The Easy Loop also has lots of links into other lines, so if you feel like moving on to something a bit more challenging, there are plenty of places to go.

Stations on the Easy Loop

Muscat, Côtes de Provence, Grenache/Garnacha Rosé, White Zinfandel, New World Rosé, Beaujolais, Red Fizz, Pink Fizz, Prosecco, Moscato.

Muscat

Muscat is not considered a glamorous or complex grape, but its simplicity and 'grapey' nature lend itself to a few different styles and a surprising change from the norm.

What you need to know

○ Muscat is a bit of an enigma – it is the only wine that consistently smells and tastes like grapes, and although it is made into dry wines as well as sweet ones, it always retains its natural fruit sweetness.

○ It's also one of the few wine grapes we can buy as eating grapes, so if you see them on the shop shelves why not try them alongside some Muscat and see if you can taste the similarities.

○ Although traditionally found in southern Europe, Muscat is now popping up all over the world. Muscat is the French name, whereas it is known as Moscato in Italy and Moscatel in Spain.

○ Muscat used to be found in half bottles as a light sweet wine, or fortified into delicious sweeties, but these days you find it increasingly as a dry French wine (Muscat sec), which is quite light, crisp and neutral with a perfumed nose.

○ You find sweet and fortified Muscat in both the Old and New World, often darker than a white wine due to the colour of the Muscat grape's skin.

Eating with Muscat

Dry Muscat is great for drinking ice-cold on a warm, sunny day. It combines a summery aroma with a thirst-quenching crispness. Light, crunchy salads, cold prawns and a garden full of pals all benefit from the addition of Muscat.

At the other end of the scale is a selection of richer fortified wines, great as an after-dinner treat. They are delicious with chocolate tarts and cheeseboards. Look out for Muscat de Rivesaltes from France or Rutherglen Muscat from Australia.

Alternatively, try Muscat de Beaumes-de-Venise, a lightly fortified sweet wine from the Rhône, in the bath or as an aperitif. Despite its heady perfume, it's actually quite light.

Visiting Muscat

Today you can find Muscat all over the world, including Italy, Spain and the US. However, I love it best from the rugged south of France, where you find the thirst-quenching Muscat sec; soft and sweet Muscat de Beaumes-de-Venise, and the fortified wines made in tiny villages as they always have been. Head for a local bar in one of the villages and sip an ice-cold Muscat while watching the locals taking part in a game of *pétanque*.

Côtes de Provence ◎

This is the palest of rosés, often so light it's hardly noticeable on the shelf. As the colour suggests, it's a delicate wine, easily overpowered. In the right company its delightful dry style, light pink colour and sunshine flavours make it a great 'afternoon in the garden' wine.

What you need to know

○ Although the region produces other wines, rosé is by far the most famous Provençal wine. It's grown in among the lavender in baking sunshine – the region gets 3000 hours of sunshine a year. This produces a crisp, dry wine with a lovely strawberry character. It needs some of that

sunshine to drink it with, too, as it never tastes quite the same on a dark miserable day.

○ Some wines have to be drunk straight from the ice bucket, and this is one of them. They don't really last either, so there's little point in hanging on to a bottle for an extra-special occasion. As soon as the sun has got its hat on, crack open the Côtes de Provence.

Eating with Côtes de Provence

Anything with very strong flavours will overpower a Côtes de Provence, so less is best: it's really for aperitifs and light bites. The crisp acidity will cut through cold meats, light cheeses and very lightly smoked salmon. I like it with cheese gougères, those lightly puffed savoury choux pastries the French make so well. Côtes de Provence isn't the cheapest of wines, so it's best to save it for lunch in the garden with a couple of friends.

Visiting Côtes de Provence

Nestled on the south-eastern coast of France, the Provence region has a rather chi-chi reputation, being home to Saint-Tropez and Nice, and prices tend to reflect that. It's also home to kilometre after kilometre of lavender fields. You're best off finding a little gîte tucked away somewhere, with a pool to enjoy your share of those 3000 hours of sunshine. Why not hire a vintage convertible (or an economy car with air-con) and cruise the country lanes, making a couple of jaunts to the sun-drenched towns? When it comes to eating out, remember that, in any town, off the main strip is where you find the local gems rather than the busy (and expensive) tourist traps.

Grenache/Garnacha Rosé

Grenache and Garnacha are the French and Spanish names for the same grape, which can also be known as Garnatxa in Catalonia and Cannonau in Sardinia. We'll call it Grenache, which is what most of the rest of the world calls it. The tricky thing about defining rosé wines when it comes to flavour is that it is relatively easy to influence the flavours and styles of grapes as you make rosé – which means you can find Grenache Rosé as the light, sweet blush style (more akin to White Zinfandel) or the big, sweeter styles (see New World Rosé). Here we are focusing on the punchy, drier rosé styles that are made across Spain and France from Grenache grapes.

What you need to know

○ Grenache features in many of the dark-pink rosés you find on the shelves, particularly from Europe – sometimes on its own, or as part of a blend (where it's a bit trickier to find the grape names mentioned).

○ The wines are intensely pink, just off-dry, and taste of delicious fresh strawberries. They have a fantastic way of filling your mouth with flavour, and then giving you a bit of a jolt with the tangy finish – a bit like sour sweets.

○ This is the rosé I stock up on when I see the beginnings of summer, as it is the most versatile and crowd-pleasing style out there. Not too sweet but not bone-dry either, I find that even men like it – even if they don't like to admit to it!

○ These wines come with many price tags and generally you get what you pay for. The cheaper wines are fine chilled down if you just fancy pink and fun; if you go up just a step though, you get a smoother wine with more flavour.

○ Great examples of Grenache are Navarra rosé from Spain and Languedoc rosé from southern France. Both are generally very reliable summer drinking.

Eating with Grenache Rosé

Because these are quite bold rosés, they work well with gutsier food and stronger flavours, and make a wonderful match for barbecues and al fresco dining. I'd happily wash down my burger, grilled lamb steaks or bowl of fat, sizzling chorizo sausages with a glass of Grenache rosé and know that the tang will cut through the oil and the bold flavours will cope with a marinade or heavy dollop of paprika. Avoid sweeter dishes or ones with a lot of chilli – the wine's tanginess will taste sour against anything sweet (like coconut milk or fresh fruit) and will turn up the chilli to a burning inferno!

Visiting Grenache Rosé

Pack your holiday togs and head to the south of France or central Spain and Catalonia (although it's available to drink all over Spain). You'll find a range of winemakers making Grenache-based wines, from the very big, more industrial sites, to the very small, unique sites. Soak up the atmosphere in some villages and towns less spoiled by tourism. Find a café-bar, order some small plates of local meats and cheeses and watch the world go by . . .

White Zinfandel

White Zinfandel or Zinfandel Blush is the softest, sweetest rosé. It is a relatively new style and has enjoyed a huge rise in popularity in the last few years, although because of its simple nature and sweet flavours it is often sniffed at in wine-drinking circles.

What you need to know

○ The style is known as 'blush' because of the wine's pale colour, which now defines the sweet taste too. Although the wine is made like a normal rosé, the juice is barely left with the red skins in order to avoid too much colour and flavour. Some sweetness is natural but there's also some added sugar – a 'blush' wine can have up to four times the amount of sugar as a dry white. So they're not good for the diet!

○ Lots of people start drinking blush wines because they are a bit sweeter, easy-going and they like the cherry and raspberry flavours. In the summer you can add lemonade or soda, ice and swizzle sticks to make a long drink for garden gatherings with friends.

Eating with White Zinfandel

The sweetness and light flavours of White Zinfandel don't make it a brilliant food match: it's best with nibbles or on its own. However, there is one area where it comes into its own – curries! In particular sweeter style, creamy curries, like chicken tikka masala. Here the sweetness of the wine balances out the curry's own sweetness, whereas a drier wine would taste sour by comparison.

This is not the wine of artisan producers and nor is it from a specific region, so visiting isn't really an option. If you were looking to base a holiday around White Zinfandel, however, then California is its spiritual home. And there are no excuses required to visit California! (*See the Zinfandel station on the Revelation Line on p. 113 for more details.*)

New World Rosé (S)

In New World wines there is a trend for dark pink, gutsy rosés. At times they are even bigger than some reds, and these are like the Yorkie bar of the rosé world. These wines come from Chile, South Africa, Australia, New Zealand and Argentina. New World Rosé can be made from any red grape, although winemakers tend to stick to globally recognised varieties such as Shiraz, Cabernet Sauvignon, Merlot, Malbec, Carmenère and Pinot Noir.

What you need to know

○ These wines are often big and boozy – they are no shrinking violets. They tend to be off-dry and bursting with flavour. Although the difference in grape, origin and producer will influence the style of wine, there is a common profile of fresh fruit flavours like strawberry, raspberry and often a bit of spice.

○ The dark colour is created by leaving the grape juice sitting with the red skins for a lot longer than traditional pale rosés. This gives them more colour, flavour and body – meaning they are more versatile than other rosés.

Eating with New World Rosé

Although these wines slip down easily with no accompaniment whatsoever, they go remarkably well with medium-spiced dishes and strong flavours. Satay, dim sum and Moroccan-style dishes can be washed down easily with a glass or two. Be careful not to have anything too spicy, however, as this will accentuate the wine's alcohol content.

Visiting New World Rosé

As with some of the other rosés, there are no clear destinations for these wines. However, I've enjoyed some fantastic times on the coast in South Africa with a glass of local rosé in hand. Repeat in Chile, Argentina, Australia, New Zealand, California and so on and I'm sure you will feel no pain.

Beaujolais ◉

These days Beaujolais is seen as a bit old-fashioned, but this soft red wine should be in your wine rack, as it's friendly and easy-going.

What you need to know

- ○ Beaujolais is a region just below the centre of France and the wines come in a variety of guises. It's not a blockbuster wine by any means, rather a soft swish in your mouth to make you smile.
- ○ It has a juicy, berry flavour, sometimes with a hint of strawberry bubblegum. The difference between Beaujolais and a lot of other red wines is it has very soft tannins, making it a light choice.
- ○ Because it's lighter it can be treated a bit differently from other red wines – you can even chill it for half an hour before you want to drink it.

○ The Beaujolais appellation has a number of levels that go from basic blends up to individual named villages like Fleurie. As you move higher up the tree, the wines develop a more complex nature but still retain their easy style.

Eating with Beaujolais
In many ways, Beaujolais acts like a white wine, even though it's red, which makes it excellent with fleshy fish, poultry and pork in simple sauces. It's also great with charcuterie and hearty salads. The more complex Cru Beaujolais wines like Fleurie, Brouilly or Morgon will all hold their own against meatier dishes.

Visiting Beaujolais
Beaujolais is a delicious mix of traditional artisan winemaking and maverick winemakers gently subverting the norm – call it Bojo rather than Boho. Like its neighbours – Burgundy to the north, and the Rhône to the south – you can happily trip from one wine-centric village to the next, more or less, avoiding commercial tourism, while gorging on simple, local dishes. Look out for vineyards offering B&B and *table d'hôte*, a fixed-price dinner which you eat literally at the host's table – a unique experience.

Red Fizz ⓢ

Many people struggle to get their heads around the concept of fizzy red wine, with its tannins and red wine flavours combined with bubbles. But it's been around for longer than people might think, originating in the Loire Valley in France and made popular by Australian winemakers in recent years.

What you need to know

- Red Fizz has been made in the Loire Valley in France for a very long time, but the relatively new wave of interest has been sparked by the Australian take on it, producing Red Fizz which is quite different from the French wines.
- Australian Red Fizz is normally made from Shiraz or Cabernet Sauvignon grapes and is a full-on mouthful with intense flavours and lots of sensations. You can get some reasonably easy-going, fruity styles (think fizzy Ribena) and others that are a bit more earthy and serious. The traditional sparkling reds from France tend to be lighter and drier, just as the French rosés differ from New World rosés.

Eating with Red Fizz

You might be amazed how Red Fizz shines when it's matched with food. It needs bold flavours and textures and, given its 'shock factor', you can be a bit shocking with the food choices. The French wines go amazingly well with charcuterie, particularly if the bottle has been dangled in a cooling river alongside your feet on a campsite. The Australian sparkling Shiraz is traditional with Christmas dinner on the beach or with a good old barbie. An alternative match is a full English brunch: Red Fizz has a real celebratory feel and the punchy flavours work so well with the meat and spices of black pudding. It's not bad with chocolate cake either!

Take your pick! How about a campsite in the Loire Valley in the height of summer, mooching from one idyllic scene to another. Or a long-haul trip to Adelaide, where the wine lands are famed for their Shiraz. Think sunshine, laidback visits to wineries and meals on the verandah.

Pink Fizz Ⓢ

Undeniably fun, Pink Fizz can come in a range of styles and prices. It's bound to cheer up a dreary evening or set the party off with a bang.

What you need to know

○ Pink Fizz is probably the most fun station on the WineTubeMap, and by creating a category to encompass all of the pink sparkling wines you can find, there is some scope for adventure.

○ There are no official classifications for Pink Fizz, but they do naturally split between fun and easy drinking, like the Italian sparklers, and the more serious stuff (well, as serious as you can get with a pink bubbly drink).

○ Like rosé wines, the pinkness does not necessarily equate to sweetness and you can get some fabulous, tangy dry wines as well as some sweeter styles.

○ If you've got a sweet tooth, try sparkling White Zinfandel. It has a high sugar content, which isn't to everyone's taste, but it's incredibly good with sweeter curries.

- For great value dry but fruity sparkling rosés, try rosé cava, Italian rosé spumante (which is no longer allowed to be called Prosecco) and some of the Australian, South American or South African rosés on the market. They share a palate of strawberry and blossom flavours, a hint of sweetness and easy-going bubbles.
- At the top end is a fantastic array of rosé Champagne-alikes, made from a blend of grapes and mostly containing Pinot Noir. These wines are more complex and normally have finer bubbles and more acidity. Many of the Champagne houses own properties in California and make very Champagne-like rosé wines.

Eating with Pink Fizz

The mid-range pink fizzes are really versatile. Good on their own or with nibbles, they can handle a fair amount of flavour and work well with lightly spiced and sweet and sour dishes. The top end of these wines are also great with food – try it as something different with smoked salmon, tempura prawns or herby salads.

Visiting Pink Fizz

Pink Fizz has no fixed abode, so it's pretty clear the party should be at yours. Crack open a bottle, invite your friends round, pump up the gramophone and have a party!

Prosecco

See the Fizz Line p. 20.

Moscato (S)

Underrated in the UK, this off-dry, frothy sparkler is quietly gaining a following around the world – which is unsurprising really, as Moscato is an absolute gem, low in alcohol and amazingly versatile. The low alcohol makes it a must if you want a treat but don't want to overdo it.

What you need to know

- The original Moscato d'Asti is from northern Italy. It is sweet without being sickly, with a lick of fresh summer fruits and a bit of blossom. It is frothy, gently sweet, low in alcohol and brilliant at bringing a smile to everyone's face.
- Technically the wines are classified as *frizzante* (lightly sparkling) rather than *spumante* (sparkling). Traditionally Moscato has low alcohol, normally under 7%, making it a very easy drink.
- You can now find Moscato being made all around the world, particularly in California and Australia, because the style is so popular. Their wines are sometimes pink, sometimes not, but always light, sweet and easy-going.
- Moscato is one of life's guilty pleasures – fact!

Eating with Moscato

There are some matches made in heaven and Moscato and meringues is one of them. They share a frothy lightness that works really well together. Moscato can make a really nice end to a dinner if you don't want to do a big pudding. Simply serve a glass with a square of white chocolate or bowl of fruit salad. Delicious.

Visiting Moscato

Visiting Moscato would traditionally involve a trip to the Piedmont region of Italy, where Moscato d'Asti is made (*see Barolo on the Rediscovery Line*). However, some of the recent Moscato revival has been credited to a growing number of hip-hop and rap stars name-checking it in their lyrics. So it might be more appropriate to head to your nearest dark, sweaty nightclub and get jiggy with it instead.

Beaujolais ◎

Valpolicella ◎

Chianti ◎

Cabernet Franc ✿

New World Pinot Noir ✿

Red Burgundy ⊕

Barolo ◎

Amarone ◎

 S   style of wine

✿   grape type

⊕   geographical
     region

◎   official name
     for a wine

5. The Rediscovery Line

The Rediscovery Line is a bit like visiting Rome: it's full of masterpieces, beautifully crafted but very much of their time. The wines on the Rediscovery Line are all classics, mostly European, but they feel like they've fallen foul to newer, 'trendier' wines. Despite this sad fall from favour, these wines can be a joy to explore, particularly if you know what to look out for and when to drink them. They are sophisticated, interesting and great with food; they are also brilliant ways of impressing people, either with a gift or with something really delicious for dinner.

When to take the Rediscovery Line
For dinner: whether it's your tea on Tuesday night or dinner to impress a prospective client, these wines won't let you down. They'll taste great and make you look great too. However, they aren't always the best choice for drinking in restaurants (unless you've got a wine guide handy and lots of spare cash) as they tend to be at the top end of the scale and can differ depending on the producer and the vintage.

Stations on the Rediscovery Line
Beaujolais, Valpolicella, Chianti, Cabernet Franc, New World Pinot Noir, Red Burgundy, Barolo, Amarone.

Beaujolais

See the Easy Loop p. 71.

Valpolicella

Valpolicella is a soft and easy-drinking style of red wine from Italy. For years it was churned out as cheap and cheerful plonk, but the locals are now carefully rebuilding the region and improving the wine's reputation.

What you need to know

○ Valpolicella is a northern Italian red from Veneto, near Verona and Lake Garda. It is made from local grapes, predominantly Corvina.

○ Simple by nature, these wines have an interesting mix of acidity and sweetness and often taste like slightly tangy cherries. This is a characteristic of many reds grown in cooler climates.

○ Because of its simplicity and lack of tannins you can chill it down for relaxed summer drinking.

○ Like most Italian wines it's not easy to work out what you're getting when you pick up a bottle of Valpolicella as there are no recognisable grape names or famous brands. Don't be seduced by very cheap bottles, because you do get what you pay for.

○ If you like Valpolicella and want to take it to the next level, look for Ripasso on the label for a fuller, richer style.

Eating with Valpolicella

This is not a big, complicated wine so it's perfect for drinking on its own or with laidback food like buffets, picnics or pizza. The acidity helps it stand up to cold meats and cheeses.

Visiting Valpolicella

Although nowhere near as famous as some of Italy's other cities, beautiful Verona is well worth exploring (*see Amarone on this line*). Why not pair up a weekend in Verona with a couple of nights in one of the wine region's up-and-coming B&Bs or working vineyards with rooms. It's an opportunity to discover some of the old and new vineyards and local food traditions in the *osterie*, olive groves and farms.

Chianti ⊙

This Italian red is a Tuscan classic, and possibly the most famous Italian wine. With its versatility and diverse range of styles, it should have a home in every wine rack.

What you need to know

○ Chianti is an Italian DOCG, located in Tuscany on the west coast of Italy. The area covered by the regulation is large and the terrain and climate differ greatly, producing many stylistic nuances.

○ Chianti is characterised by a fragrant dark cherry flavour with hints of spice. The wines are smooth and round with a bite of dry tannin on the finish.

○ Chianti must be at least 80% Sangiovese and is blended with a combination of other grapes.

- In terms of classification, Chianti Riserva means that the wine has spent a significantly longer spell in oak, giving it more subtle fruit and greater spiciness and nuttiness. Superiore means that it has passed more stringent quality controls, resulting in more alcohol and a drier wine with more flavours as a general rule.
- If you like Chianti and want to throw caution to the wind, you could invest in a 'super Tuscan'. These are the new breed of blockbuster wines from some of the top producers in Chianti. They don't necessarily stick to the rule book so aren't called Chianti, but they are the most amazing wines and are distinctively Tuscan flavoured. Just be prepared to spend a lot of money!

Eating with Chianti
Chianti proves the 'match local' rule: it works brilliantly with tomato sauces, pasta drenched in olive oil and cold meat, antipasto style. The Riservas can handle meatier dishes such as sausage casserole.

Visiting Chianti
Known as Chianti-shire in some circles because of its popularity with the Brits, this area is more beautiful than a picture postcard. Set between Florence and Siena, it is easy to access and is a dream of trattorias and free vineyard tours. However, there are parts of this region that are over-developed and lacking in character, so do your homework to find the real heart of Tuscany.

Cabernet Franc

This is a name that you rarely see on the front of a bottle, but it's the main grape in a number of French classics and the secret weapon in many blends. Cabernet Franc is probably not going to become a major part of your life, but it might turn up more often than you think.

What you need to know

- A red grape, traditionally grown in the Loire Valley in France and found in wines like Bourgeuil and Chinon, as well as a blend enhancer in Bordeaux and Bordeaux-style wines all over the world.
- It has a lighter character than many reds; in a good wine you should get a hint of violets over fresh raspberry and blackcurrant flavours. It often has a 'crunch', which is very refreshing.
- Chilean Cabernet Francs are often a bit less crunchy and a bit juicier, making them easy to drink without food.
- At times Cabernet Franc can be a bit bitter and the wine can seem a little too dry. New World growers go out of their way to avoid this, whereas the French sometimes seem to quite like it.
- It is one of the few reds that you don't want to serve warm. Pop it in the fridge for half an hour before you want to drink it – you'll enjoy the crunchiness!

Eating with Cabernet Franc

This wine goes really well with light, slightly fatty meats, particularly pork, whether it is roasted belly, charcuterie or gammon. It's also very good with simple grilled red meat like lamb steaks with ratatouille.

Visiting Cabernet Franc

Hire a cottage for a few days near the town of Chinon in the Loire Valley. The wineries aren't far from each other, so you can cycle or even stroll to them, leaving you without the problem of who's driving and instead with the issue of carrying the bottles! Chinon itself is a bustling town on the banks of the River Vienne, with a weekly market and a castle.

New World Pinot Noir

Pinot Noir is a darling of the wine world, and the New World reimagined version of Red Burgundy has a style all of its own.

What you need to know

- Pinot Noir is notoriously difficult to grow, which is why it is far less available (and therefore more expensive) than other grapes. Outside its classic home of Burgundy, it flourishes in New Zealand, California, Oregon, Chile, Australia and Romania as well as other pockets of cool climate.
- Although styles can differ, Pinot Noir is known for its medium body, evocative perfume and silky tannins and acidity. What it lacks in body it makes up for in pungency.
- With these wines you often taste raspberries or the fruits on top of Black Forest gateaux, often laced with an indescribable muskiness.
- Not everyone likes it, however, and you can come across quite a lot of anti-Pinot Noir snobbery!

Eating with New World Pinot Noir

Because of its lighter style, Pinot Noir is one of the red wines that can be chilled slightly and is good with food traditionally matched with white wines. It is a great fish wine, from smoked salmon to monkfish tails. It's also a good rule of thumb to drink New World Pinot Noir with meats that go well with a berry sauce, particularly duck.

Visiting New World Pinot Noir

This is a toss-up between Central Otago in New Zealand and Oregon on the west coast of the US. Wine aficionados will argue which produces the best Pinot Noir, while you can decide which is the best to visit. Central Otago is a rugged inland area of New Zealand's South Island, with an outdoorsy and laidback style. Hike, bike, fish, eat, drink or just marvel at the scenery. You'll come back healthier than you left! While Oregon isn't as 'hot' as California, it does have a thriving food and drink scene. Base yourself in up-and-coming Portland and travel the Willamette Valley, where the best Pinot Noirs are grown.

Red Burgundy

Burgundy has an expensive and confusing reputation, making it a difficult wine to explore. But a good Red Burgundy is an experience not to be missed.

What you need to know

○ Red Burgundy is almost always made using the Pinot Noir grape and has a lighter body than many reds. The wines have a fragrant raspberry and redcurrant flavour, and many of them also have an earthiness (in some cases called 'farmyardy') which is very typical, but not loved by all.

○ There are many appellations within Red Burgundy, from plain 'Bourgogne' to Montrachet Grand Cru. The classification is geographical and refers to a specific site and the quality of the grapes grown there. Because of this, it can be very hard to navigate and understand what you're getting for your money. Essentially Bourgogne is the simplest appellation, followed by the generic wines from Côte de Beaune or Côte de Nuits. After that the wines are named after villages (like Puligny or Pommard), then the Premier Crus and Grand Crus are deemed to be from specific vineyards or a blend of specific vineyards – phew!

○ If you're keen to explore, start off with some wines like Hautes-Côte de Beaune or Côte de Nuits, which are good quality without breaking the bank, or try a lesser known (and therefore cheaper) appellation like Rully or Ladoix.

Eating with Red Burgundy

The rule of thumb doesn't differ massively from New World Pinot Noir: this is an ambidextrous grape, able to cope with fish, white meats and red meats. Where New World Pinot Noir delivers a fruit bomb, Red Burgundy is more savoury so it works well with game dishes and earthy flavours like mushrooms, caramelised meats, onions and woody herbs.

Visiting Red Burgundy

As with White Burgundy, the options for Red Burgundy allow you to visit some of the villages and towns of the region, sampling the micro culture of each one in a traditional way. They are not overly touristy in the main, and a camping holiday in the summer, with hired bikes to explore the vineyards and to collect some local goodies from the market, would be an excellent way to explore.

Barolo ◉

An intense Italian red wine which is unusually fragrant and not always easy to understand.

What you need to know
- ○ Barolo is dark, tannic and needs time. It is made to be aged and drinking it young can be quite a challenge. Modern winemaking softens the tannins, which helps, but don't expect to glug this back.
- ○ The wine is made from the Nebbiolo grape and has an intense flavour and perfume: it is less fruity and more savoury than many wines – mushroom or truffle and black coffee are common descriptions of the aroma, with dried fruit on the palate.
- ○ It is high in everything – alcohol, tannins, acidity and oak – which is why it needs time to soften the edges and for all of those things to meld together.
- ○ Barolo is never cheap, but you can get good ones at the lower end of the budget if you do a bit of research, and it's a great way to impress the wine snobs in your life. Be canny when you're shopping: if you have good will power a younger wine which isn't quite ready to drink might be better value, but if you have low will power, seek out one that is a few years old and is ready to drink now!

Eating with Barolo
Because of the big structure and high levels of acidity and tannins, Barolo is not a wine for drinking on its own. It really needs to accompany food, and the foods of its home in northern Italy are the perfect foil – think mushroom risotto, truffles and sticky stews. It's also pretty amazing with a good steak.

Visiting Barolo

The Langhe region at the foot of the Alps is a gourmet delight, home to truffles, cheeses, risottos and many types of pasta. If you visit in autumn you will see the vines at harvest time when the leaves turn red. It's also the best time to visit if you want to experience truffle season.

Amarone ◎

A serious wine! It sounds good, most people have heard of it, and it can't fail to impress.

What you need to know

○ A high-quality DOCG within the Valpolicella appellation (in northern Italy) and formally known as Amarone della Valpolicella, this is the daddy of wines.

○ The grapes are picked late and are then laid out to dry (traditionally on straw mats) in order to let the sugars and flavours intensify as the grapes shrivel into almost raisins. This means that the juice is concentrated and sweet when the grapes are pressed, and makes for wines that are strong (a minimum alcohol content of 14%) and voluptuous. It is then barrel-aged once it's finally made.

○ Amarone is a rich red wine, like black cherries and raisins dipped in dark chocolate. Unlike the Valpolicella wines, this has low acidity and lower tannins.

○ Valpolicella Ripasso is a sort of stepping stone between Amarone and Valpolicella, using the Amarone skins to enhance a younger Valpolicella.

Eating with Amarone

This is such a rich wine, and you need to be feeling a bit rich to buy a bottle, so the accompanying food needs to merit the wine. The lower tannins mean that it's great with slow-cooked meats, like braised beef shin, or a pie full of braised game. It's also a really nice wine for a cheeseboard, as its lower acidity makes it great to sip and savour after a meal. Just beware of the headache the next day!

Visiting Amarone

Amarone and Valpolicella are made in the same areas – sometimes in the same wineries – but if Valpolicella is about rustic charm, Amarone is its sophisticated cousin. So after visiting the vineyards, head to Verona, a charming city that doesn't get the same fanfare as neighbouring Venice but is just as deserving. Take your time to soak up the atmosphere in the medieval streets, check out the bronze of Shakespeare's Juliet and soak up some culture at the opera in the stunning Roman arena.

Côtes de Provence

Grenache/Garnacha Rosé

White Zinfandel

New World Rosé

Beaujolais

Valpolicella

Chianti

Cabernet Franc

New World Pinot Noir

Rhône

Languedoc

Grenache/Garnacha

Shiraz/Syrah

Cabernet Sauvignon

Bordeaux

Rioja

Douro

 style of wine

grape type

geographical region

official name for a wine

6. The Red Central Line

The Red Central Line is all-encompassing, moving from pink and light reds through the heartland of red wine, with classic regions and grapes. If you know this line then you'll have most of your drinking occasions sorted, whether it's summer picnics, Christmas dinner or impressing your new romantic interest. The wines share the characteristics of vibrant fruitiness, ranging from fresh strawberries to baked blackcurrants, with the influence of oak ageing, tannins and spiciness growing as you travel along the line.

When to take the Red Central Line
When not to? This line has it all. It's mostly a foodie line, but one which can handle the pace regardless of what you're eating. It will impress your friends and wine snobs alike.

Stations on the Red Central Line
Côtes de Provence, Grenache/Garnacha Rosé, White Zinfandel, New World Rosé, Beaujolais, Valpolicella, Chianti, Cabernet Franc, New World Pinot Noir, Rhône, Languedoc, Grenache/Garnacha, Shiraz/Syrah, Cabernet Sauvignon, Bordeaux, Rioja, Douro.

Côtes de Provence

See the Easy Loop p. 65.

Grenache / Garnacha Rosé

See the Easy Loop p. 67.

White Zinfandel

See the Easy Loop p. 69.

New World Rosé

See the Easy Loop p. 70.

Beaujolais

See the Easy Loop p. 71.

Valpolicella

See the Rediscovery Line p. 80.

Chianti

See the Rediscovery Line p. 81.

Cabernet Franc

See the Rediscovery Line p. 83.

New World Pinot Noir

See the Rediscovery Line p. 84.

Rhône

This is a small word for a big area, where they make a rich red
for every occasion. The north and the south of the Rhône are
very different and this station is all about the southern reds.
Although there are lots of different wines within the region,
they share some family features.

What you need to know

- The wines of the Rhône are some of the most versatile and best value foodie wines out there. They are a great go-to in restaurants and stalwarts in the wine rack.
- The wines are all named after geographical areas and the higher up the quality tree you go, the more specific (and smaller) the area is.
- Most of the wines are based on a blend of Grenache with Syrah (Shiraz) and other local grapes added in for interest. Because they are blends they tend to be round and smooth. A blend means the winemaker takes the best bit of different grapes and puts them together to make a whole.
- Côtes du Rhône is the most produced wine from the region, which is why it is often cheaper and more widely available.
- If you like Côtes du Rhône, look out for 'Villages' on the labels or wines called Vacqueyras or Gigondas. 'Villages' on the label means the wines can only come from selected villages which are deemed to produce 'better' wine, and Vacqueyras and Gigondas are village names. Wines from these two villages have more character and tend to be a bit more serious.
- Châteauneuf-du-Pape could have a whole chapter of its own. The area in which it can be produced is small and the conditions are very specific, which is why Châteauneuf-du-Pape has a unique, rich fruitcake flavour. It's special, but you do pay for it!

Eating with Rhône

Because there is such a spread in quality and price, you could have a Rhône wine every day of the week. All of the wines have got lots of fruit and tannins so can match hearty foods and flavours like herby sausages, game and, of course, roast beef with all the trimmings.

Visiting the Rhône

Like many other wine areas of France, when you get there you realise that there aren't any major signposts, visitor centres or tourist attractions. There are the amazing ruins of Châteauneuf-du-Pape on the banks of the river, and the village has a quaint hotel on the square with views out across the vineyards (but not much else!). If you like culture then visit Avignon, a lovely city, close enough to visit the vineyards and still get your dose of art and restaurants.

Languedoc

The beautiful, sunny south of France produces a myriad of red wines and the Languedoc contains some of the wines that most epitomise the area. They are full-bodied but soft round the edges and a bit rustic, just like the region itself.

What you need to know

- These wines warm your cockles, and seem to work on a crisp autumnal day just as well as in the warm summer months.
- Because of all the lovely sunshine, the flavours are rich and ripe, the tannins and alcohol big but soft and, to top it off, you often get a whiff of the Garrigue, the herbaceous scrub land that surrounds the vineyards.
- Most wines from the Languedoc are blended from a mixture of local grapes like Carignan and more well-known grapes like Grenache.
- The area contains a range of appellations: Fitou, Minervois, Corbières, Saint-Chinian and Pic Saint-Loup to name but a few. They all differ but have enough similarities to group them together.

- There is also an AC Languedoc – not a football team but a catch-all appellation, a bit like Côtes du Rhône.
- Fitou and Corbières are probably the most easy-going wines from the region, whereas Saint-Chinian and Pic Saint-Loup are a bit more serious.

Eating with Languedoc
Languedoc wines go particularly well with grilled and charred meat or vegetables and anything with take-no-prisoners herby marinades. It's also a star performer with meaty sausages.

Visiting Languedoc
This expansive area in the south of France is a fascinating place to visit. Whether you are a history buff or not, you can't fail to be sucked in by the ancient city of Carcassonne and hilltop Cathar fortress. Back in the modern day, Narbonne is a bustling city with a great indoor food market and lovely river to sit by, sipping a glass of wine, and once you're fed up of the city you can always hit the nearby beach.

Grenache / Garnacha

This grape has long been a stalwart of Spanish and French winemaking. Often hidden away in blends in the past, now this classic grape is beginning to appear as the solo artist on many labels around the world.

What you need to know

O Grenache/Garnacha appears in some of the world's top wines – including Chateauneuf-du-Pape and Priorat, as part of a blend with other grapes – however, it's definitely worth a try in its own right.

O You'll find it most abundantly as Garnacha from Spain – juicy, bright and easy-drinking – or from Australia, where it packs a bigger punch. Those aged in oak tend to develop a velvety richness.

O It is often lower in tannins than some of the firmer reds, which makes it both soft and powerful, with a punchy alcohol content. This is partly because it grows well in extreme heat, resulting in very ripe grapes with a high sugar content, which converts to alcohol during the process.

O Grenache is a flamboyant kind of grape, with lots of woohoo flavour, but less substance. It's a particularly good wine for people who don't like drying tannins.

O It nearly made it on to the Revelation Line . . . but the flavours are less dark and brooding and a bit more red: think plums and strawberries.

O Because Grenache grows quite abundantly, it's also often a great bargain!

Eating with Grenache/Garnacha

Because Grenache/Garnacha is lower in tannins, it isn't your ideal steak wine, but its pungent flavour makes it good with in-your-face food like gourmet burgers and pizzas. The more serious aged wines work brilliantly with slow-cooked meats and stews.

Visiting Grenache/Garnacha

You could visit Barossa (*see Syrah/Shiraz*) for a taste of Grenache, but closer to home is the region of Priorat, two hours south of Barcelona. This area, set in the shadow of the Montsant mountain range, isn't a particularly touristy area. It's a rocky landscape, peppered with tiny vineyards and olive groves where the influence of the Moors is still visible. So if you fancy a relaxed trip where you can dip into Moorish history, taste wine and olive oil and do a bit of hiking and sauntering in local villages, then this could be the place for you.

Shiraz / Syrah

This grape has a dual personality, traditionally using the name Syrah in France and Shiraz in Australia. However, you will be able to find both names used in most countries. It plays a major role in some of the world's greatest red wines as well as the cheapest red blends.

What you need to know

○ The grapes make powerful, full-bodied, spicy and alcoholic red or rosé wines. You mostly get juicy blackberry and roasted spice flavours, often with hints of chocolate and coffee enhanced by the use of oak.

- With these wines, you get what you pay for. At the lower end you get soft, sweet wines (a bit like Ribena) and at the upper end you get elegant, complex, sophisticated wines with more tannin and structure.
- The best Shiraz/Syrah is traditionally found in Australia's Barossa Valley and McLaren Vale, and the northern Rhône in France, in wines like Côte-Rôtie and Saint-Joseph.

Eating with Shiraz/Syrah

There are so many styles of Syrah/Shiraz that it's difficult to pin it down, although it's generally a big wine so it's not for light dishes. With the in-your-face, soft, easy styles go for food that is similar – think fancy burgers, bangers and mash or a meaty tagine. Sirloin steak or classic roast beef make a great match for a more refined Syrah/Shiraz. Of course it's not just beef: the more subtle styles of the wines work really well with lamb and duck dishes. I'm also partial to a drop with well-cooked venison, as the combination of berry and spice makes a perfect match for this wine.

Visiting Shiraz/Syrah

You could go anywhere in the world to visit these wines, but head to Barossa for a trip to the heart of Shiraz. An hour's drive from Adelaide in South Australia, it is a hotbed of food and culture with bustling little towns, vast expanses of land and big sky. Barossa is geared up for visitors too, so you can get around and find out what's going on easily, whether it's a farmers' market, art gallery, wine tour or cricket match.

Cabernet Sauvignon

One of the world's most classic grapes, Cabernet Sauvignon can be found growing in every wine-producing country, in the vineyards of both the premium and the industrial producers.

What you need to know

○ Blackcurrants! It's the classic flavour of Cabernet Sauvignon (commonly referred to as Cab Sauv) and, despite its prolific nature and ability to blend with other grapes, you can still taste the blackcurrants.

○ Cabernet Sauvignon flourishes in so many places, sometimes blended with other grapes, like in Bordeaux, and sometimes on its own. It is a flagship grape in Napa and Sonoma in California, Coonawarra in South Australia and in the warmer parts of Chile. In each area it manages to take on the local style while retaining its distinctive character.

○ Cabernet Sauvignon is one of the more 'structured' grapes. Not only does it have a lot of flavour, it also has backbone, giving it tannin and an ability to age. You often find older vintages and some serious barrel ageing.

○ Because it is so well recognised around the world, Cabernet Sauvignon is a popular grape to make cheaper wine with too. At the budget end of the spectrum it's all about the blackcurrant, resulting in a juicy wine with some tannins. As you go up the scale and pay a bit more, you get layers of flavour and much more sophistication. Depending on how and where the wine is made you might taste black olives, liquorice and even mint – this is a distinctive Cabernet Sauvignon trait.

Eating with Cabernet Sauvignon

Cabernet Sauvignon's structure can be a bit overwhelming with food. Although you might think steak is a great option – and it isn't a bad one – actually dishes with a bit more complexity work well with the layers of flavour in this grape. Braised beef with creamy mash and vegetables, venison and juniper or a meaty duck dish would all do the trick.

Visiting Cabernet Sauvignon

You could go anywhere in the world to visit Cabernet Sauvignon. Napa and Sonoma are the obvious choice (*see Chardonnay*), as is Coonawarra in South Australia, halfway between Melbourne and Adelaide. Take the Great Ocean Road if you have time, stopping off to explore the national parks, rainforests, sand dunes and lots of exotic wildlife. Or perhaps head to Chile and visit Valparaiso. Dubbed Latin America's most unusual city, it is both gritty and bohemian and a great base from which to discover some of Chile's most famous vineyard areas.

Bordeaux ◉

A serious, sophisticated red. Often associated with Claret and the upper classes, this is a delicious style and a great food wine.

What you need to know

○ Bordeaux is a beautiful town on the River Garonne in the west of France. Like so many French wines, the Bordeaux appellation is split into lots of sub-regions, each of which has its own unique characteristics.

- Most Bordeaux is a blend of Merlot, Cabernet Sauvignon and Cabernet Franc. The quantities depend on the winemaker, the area and the weather conditions.
- Bordeaux wines tend to be full-bodied with lots of tannins and structure, but they also have plenty of intense fruit flavours.
- The two most famous regions are Saint-Émilion, which traditionally has more Merlot in the blend and is generally rounder, fruitier and softer, and Médoc, which is predominantly Cabernet Sauvignon, resulting in a wine with more tannins, more structure and which normally ages better.
- Bordeaux has a heritage of chateaux and some of these carry a price tag to rival fashion houses. However, Bordeaux Supérieur is a step up from basic Bordeaux (if you can call it basic) and often offers really good value.
- Traditionally wine merchants sold their Bordeaux wines as *en primeur*, which is a specific way of buying wine as an investment, like futures. You buy and pay for the wine while it is still in barrel, long before it is ready to drink, and receive it much later. You do need to know what you're looking for if you are planning to do this, and although some other wines are sold *en primeur*, it is most common in Bordeaux.

Eating with Bordeaux

There is a lot of variety in Bordeaux wines, but they do share a need for food, as without something to eat the tannins are too dry. Roast lamb, game stew and steak are all good matches, as are some softer cheeses like Camembert.

Visiting Bordeaux

Bordeaux is a lovely city to visit, smart and sophisticated with stunning river views. The surrounding chateaux are a sight to behold and well worth visiting, even if you can't afford the wines. Or if you are the sporty type, why not run the Médoc marathon, where producers line the route handing out samples!

Rioja ◉

A favourite in a lot of households, these wines have the body, silkiness and flavours to seduce you.

What you need to know

○ Rioja is made in the beautiful region of the same name in the northern part of Spain, from a blend of principally Tempranillo grapes.

○ The wines are well known for the use of oak and the trademark vanilla style it imparts to the otherwise full-bodied and fruity red.

○ Traditionally the wines were aged for such a long time that they lost a lot of flavour and freshness, resulting in a wine that tasted of nothing but oak. There is now a much more modern style of winemaking that focuses on enhancing the fresh berry flavours and combining it with some oak, and these are much easier wines to drink and to eat with.

○ Rioja has a system of classifying wines which dictates how old they are and how much oak ageing they have undergone: Joven, Crianza, Reserva and Gran Reserva. The Joven is the fruitiest, with little or no ageing, while at the other end of the spectrum the Gran Reserva will have spent at least two years in oak barrels and three more in the bottle afterwards, creating a complex and layered wine.

Eating with Rioja

Rioja is a pretty versatile red wine, with lots of flavour and a bit of silkiness. This means you can be quite bold with your pairings. Safe bets are lamb dishes, meaty braises and steaks; slightly bolder options are hearty fish dishes like monkfish stew or cod wrapped in pancetta.

Visiting Rioja

Rioja is a stunning region to visit, particularly at harvest time in the autumn, when the temperature becomes a bit more comfortable, the leaves are turning and there is a buzz of activity in the vineyard. Alongside the traditional, Rioja is home to some of the most cutting-edge and architectural wineries. These cathedrals to wine are not to be missed and pepper the skyline with unthinkable shapes. Stay in the towns of Haro and Logroño where you can wander the streets lined with tapas bars (*see White Rioja*) and soak up the atmosphere.

Douro

The Portuguese have been making red wine alongside their famous Port for a long time. Recently the Douro wines have been garnering more attention, and these days most wine shops and supermarkets will have at least some in their range.

What you need to know

- The River Douro winds through the hills of Portugal, creating a very unusual landscape for winemaking. The vineyards are cut into the hillsides and wind along the curves of the river.
- Douro is made using a similar blend of grapes to Port, most of which are unheard-of in the rest of the world. The most common are Touriga Nacional and Tinta Roriz (which is actually Tempranillo). It is often the Port houses themselves which release the table wines as well as their fortified cousins.
- The wines can be medium to full-bodied, with lots of dark fruit flavours like blackcurrants and blackberries, and often a sweet hint of vanilla or chocolate.

Eating with Douro

Like many of the wines on this line, Douro is a great food matcher, working well with lamb, beef and game. The extra acidity over Rioja means you can also pair Douro with tomato-based stews and cold meats.

Visiting Douro

The Douro Valley is an incredible place, and particularly good to visit in late spring when the temperature is ideal for exploring. Oporto is situated at the mouth of the river and is a UNESCO World Heritage site well worth a visit, and on the opposite side of the river is Vila Nova de Gaia, where much of the Port is still stored in barrels. However, for a real taste of the wine region it's best to travel upstream to the towns of Regua and Pinhão.

Malbec 🍇

Carmenère 🍇

Ribera del Duero ◎

Merlot 🍇

Primitivo/Zinfandel 🍇

Shiraz/Syrah 🍇

Coffee style Ⓢ

Ⓢ style of wine

🍇 grape type

🌐 geographical
    region

◎ official name
   for a wine

7. The Revelation Line

The Revelation Line is about wines that are a bit different (if you know where to look). They are inky-dark, velvety and pack a punch, both in flavour and body. Some of the wines are commonplace, like Merlot; some are rising stars, like Malbec and Carmenère; and some are on the edge of our vision, like Coffee Style. The thing about these is that you need to know what you're looking for, but with a bit of research you'll get more than you bargained for.

When to take the Revelation Line
When you're feeling brave! Most of these wines are full-bodied and high in alcohol, and are best consumed with something meaty to mop them up. That said, they can have a silky velvetiness that makes them easy to sip – just watch out for that headache the next day!

Stations on the Revelation Line
Malbec, Carmenère, Ribera del Duero, Merlot, Primitivo/Zinfandel, Shiraz/Syrah, Coffee Style

Malbec

An increasing favourite among red wine drinkers, hailing from beautiful Argentina.

What you need to know

O Although originally French, Malbec has become the signature grape of Argentina and a lot of its recent popularity is because of Argentinean development of the grape.

O Malbec is inky-dark and velvety, with a plum and blackcurrant signature flavour.

O In Cahors (south-west France), where Malbec reigns supreme, the wines produced are so dark they are known as the 'black' wines, and have incredibly high tannins.

O In Argentina, and the countries now planting Malbec to create similar wines, the tannins are softer and richer, making the wine much more appealing. Look for wines from the Uco Valley, high in the hills in Mendoza (Argentina's principal wine-growing area). They are the best of the best.

O The use of barrels can transform Malbec, changing a fairly juicy and fun red into a more serious, drier food wine.

Eating with Malbec

Malbec is a stalwart of the wine rack. The classic food match is an Argentinean steak (what else!), but you could also try it with spicy Mexican food, robust sausages or even on its own – especially the lighter, unoaked styles.

Visiting Malbec

You would have to go to Argentina to get a real flavour of Malbec. Buenos Aires is a hotbed of food and culture and the tango is still alive and kicking. But don't spend all your time in Buenos Aires: in wine country, Mendoza is a vibrant town surrounded by extreme outdoor activities, incredible views and great wines to taste.

Carmenère

The spy of the grape world, Carmenère had been living undercover in Chile until recently. This medium-bodied and flavour-packed red is experiencing a surge of popularity – and rightly so.

What you need to know

○ Carmenère is to Chile what Malbec is to Argentina: an adopted local hero that flourishes in its host country's climate.

○ The wines are incredibly versatile – often a mix of rich berries, chocolate and sometimes a hint of green pepper.

○ The Carmenère grape travelled to Chile from France and was planted with Merlot where, for many years, the two were considered to be the same. In 1994 it was confirmed that the two grapes were in fact different and the stand-alone Chilean Carmenère was born.

○ There is a big jump in quality between the cheapest Carmenères and the next level up. Pay a bit more and you'll get a great-value wine, worth much more than the price tag.

Eating with Carmenère

These wines are great with food and do well with loads of easy dishes like lasagne, pork chops or a minute steak. But the most interesting thing by far is how well it goes with Madras curries – there's a natural affinity between the two.

Visiting Carmenère

Chile is a diverse country to visit, with desert and glaciers, mountains and coastline. The people are friendly and there are some super wineries where you can stay, soak up the atmosphere and explore the wines. While you're there you can take in a polo match, the national sport!

Ribera del Duero ⊚

A cool-blooded red wine, situated between Douro and Rioja and bang on trend right now.

What you need to know

○ Ribera del Duero is a modern wine appellation only a couple of hours from Rioja. The wines only really entered the world stage in the 1990s, although wine was made in the region 2000 years ago.

○ It is a fresh style of red wine, mostly made from the Tempranillo grape, although Cabernet Sauvignon, Malbec, Merlot and Garnacha are sometimes blended in. The big difference from Rioja is that the grapes are grown at altitude, giving them bright acidity and a crunchy freshness. The wines are medium-bodied and oak-aged, so you get lots of ripe berry flavours, vanilla and spice.

○ Vega Sicilia is the iconic producer of the region and, along with other key producers, has pushed the reputation and quality of this wine forward (and the price up!).

Eating with Ribera del Duero

Like many modern red wines, this is great with meaty dishes. The bright acidity goes well with rich sauces, so think about pairing it with something like venison steak with a bold jus, or the local speciality, lamb.

Visiting Ribera del Duero

Valladolid is a bustling Spanish town and, like so many cities across Spain, has a thriving tapas scene. Base yourself here to visit a number of wineries, ranging from state-of-the-art architecture to ancient cellars. The area has castles and monasteries galore, so you can brush up on Spanish history as well as the wines.

Merlot

Merlot is velvety and soft, making it a great quaffing wine as well as being a major part of some of the world's great blends.

What you need to know

○ Merlot turns up all over the place as both an easy-drinking single varietal and a serious wine, mostly as part of a blend like Bordeaux.

○ It's known for its almost purple colour, plummy flavours, natural sweetness and soft tannins.

○ Over the years its easy nature has been exploited and you find it on the front label of brands from all over the world. Unfortunately they don't always do a great job and the result can be sweet and sickly.

- Merlot is the main grape in many Bordeaux and Bordeaux-style wines, adding a silky texture to the sometimes hard-edged Cabernet Sauvignon. You'll find it is predominant in wines from Saint-Émilion.
- Chile and California are both known for their Merlots. At the cheaper end they are jammy and ripe, but if you pay a bit extra you get a more sophisticated wine.

Eating with Merlot

Merlot is a relaxed grape: it doesn't need anything too complicated or fancy to pair with it. Think of it as a perfect partner for the sofa, when you want a warm, comforting glass of red to go with some nibbles, your tea or just to drink on its own.

Visiting Merlot

This is another global grape with no fixed abode. You could go to Bordeaux, Chile or California. Chile seems to be the home of a Merlot that isn't as bold and broad as Californian nor as structured as Bordeaux. So why not head to Santiago in Chile? You need to delve a bit to get past the financial centre, but you'll be rewarded with culture, art and lots of food.

Primitivo / Zinfandel

A slightly confused, bouncy red wine with two names, two homes and two heritages.

What you need to know
- Primitivo or Zinfandel is a red wine grape. It was believed to be two different grapes until the 1970s, when it was discovered that it's actually one and the same.
- Normally you find Zinfandel (or 'Zin') grown in California, and it is considered to be the 'signature' grape of the US.
- Primitivo turns up in the Puglia region in the heel of Italy and is becoming more fashionable due to the Zin link.
- While there are distinct differences between the two wines, both have a high level of alcohol and deep brambly flavour.
- Californian Zin tends to be softer, with jammy, juicy flavours and often sweet vanilla oak. It's also the source of the pink 'blush' wines. Primitivo is much more robust, with high tannins and intense flavours.

Eating with Primitivo/Zinfandel
This wine is an interesting one to match, and the provenance does make a difference. Zinfandel goes really well with dishes with some sweetness to them, like tagine and cous cous. Primitivo on the other hand is great with meatier textures, like burgers with blue cheese.

Visiting Primitivo/Zinfandel
California or Italy – it's your call! The Paso Robles region in California is just off Route 1, the coastal road that runs from San Francisco to Los Angeles. It's a crazy place with an annual Zinfandel festival and no winey airs and graces, and it's a great place to discover Zin. Or head to the island of Sicily and the

Puglia region in the heel of Italy, which are magical places to visit. They are hot in the summer and mostly people still take siestas to avoid the sweltering heat. They're more rural and less touristy than other parts of Italy, but more authentic, packed with ancient history, olive groves and local tavernas. Just don't forget the phrase book!

Shiraz / Syrah   Ⓢ

See the Red Central Line p. 98.

Coffee Style   Ⓢ

A slightly off-the-wall category that's growing in popularity (and controversy), but it's a lot of fun. Imagine dipping dark fruits like cherries and plums into coffee and dark chocolate and then barbecuing it in the late summer sunshine – now imagine that in a glass!

What you need to know

○ Coffee Style has its origins in South Africa, where winemakers experimented with use of yeasts and toasted oak to accentuate the 'barrel ferment' style.

○ Because of the South African roots, the real coffee styling is often linked to the indigenous Pinotage grape, but you now also see versions with Shiraz and Cabernet Sauvignon.

○ There are a handful of wines with 'coffee' on the front label but it's not very common: you're more likely to get a hint from a wine with a name alluding to coffee, mocha or chocolate.

Eating with Coffee Style
This is a tricky match, as it will easily overwhelm subtle dishes, so big up the flavours and try it with pulled pork, braised ribs or savoury dishes with dark chocolate in the sauce. Alternatively try it with vanilla ice cream!

Visiting Coffee Style
A trip to South Africa is on the cards here, where in the course of a week you can visit cosmopolitan Cape Town or an elephant reserve on the Garden Route and do a whole lot of wine tourism. Stellenbosch is the closest wine region to Cape Town and there are also some little gems tucked away. Hire a car and explore!

Food Matching

Why bother to match your wine to what you are eating? For me, you bother because you want to get the best out of both the food and the wine and enhance the overall experience. As with everything wine-related, there's no right or wrong and it's all down to personal taste, although some foods can ruin a wine, and vice versa.

As taste is such a personal thing, both literally and in a sartorial sense, it's easy to see why can be tricky to match together food and wines in a combination that works for everyone. If you don't like seafood it doesn't matter how good a match Sauvignon Blanc is, you're probably not going to like it. Equally if you don't enjoy big red wines then Cabernet Sauvignon may not be your wine match of choice for roast beef.

Just like cooking and fashion there are some really good guiding principles – rules that generally mean you won't end up with a bad taste in your mouth. There are also some classic pairings (the equivalent of a denim jeans and a crisp cotton shirt) which are great places to start. Equally there are some really irreverent things you can do, which shouldn't work, but just do!

So that's what we've got here: the guiding principles of food matching as an entrée followed by a host of main dishes each with some classic pairings, shocking combinations and hazard signs. After that it's down to you to experiment and come up with your own recipes for matches made in heaven.

Think about flavours, not food groups. It's all too easy to say that something goes well with chicken or pasta for example, but roast chicken with all the trimmings is completely different from Thai chicken curry or chicken wings in Cajun spices. Spaghetti carbonara or lasagne? The only similarity is the pasta! In order to enhance them you need to look for completely different wine qualities. The wine choice needs to be matched to the big flavours in the dish, not the main ingredient.

Do a boxing style weigh-in! You need to have wines that are evenly matched to the food in terms of weight, otherwise one completely overpowers the other. Think about the texture of the food in the mouth. Is it big and chewy or delicate and light? Your accompanying wine needs to have a similar style.

Spicy food is notoriously difficult to match wine with. The heat of the chilli dominates the palate and reduces many wines to vinegar in the mouth. Accepted wisdom is that an off-dry wine with more of an aromatic character works well, the hint of sweetness offsetting the chilli. This is true with Thai, Chinese and Vietnamese cuisine as well as more experimental fusion dishes.

Acidity is really key. It's like a refresher for your mouth and works well with food that is naturally oily or very acidic. And it's not just white wines either – red wines with good levels of acidity make great food matches. And sparkling wines! Acidity is one of the many reasons why Champagne is a great wine to drink with food. Conversely, low-acidity wines have a habit of fading away to nothing when they are paired with a lot of foods, although spicy food is one example of where lower-acidity wines can work.

Drinking order. Some people say you should drink the right wine with the right course, and even in the days when 'formal' dining is less common, you tend to start with lighter wines with nibbles and starters, moving on to the chunkier stuff with the main course and then a sweet or fortified wine with dessert or cheese. Other people say that you should start with your best wine and then gradually go down in quality – which is good advice but how do you reconcile the two? My recommendation is that if you have gone to the trouble of choosing different wines for different courses then that's what you should have, regardless. If you are planning to drink something special midway through your evening, take it easy: alcohol inhibits your ability to taste so you'll not get the most of your wine if you've already had a few! You can give yourself a chance by cleansing your palate with some sparkling water. Or save the special wine for a day where you open it at the beginning of the meal.

Going local. Traditionally you were always advised to drink wine from the same region as the food, on the basis that culturally and climatically the two have grown to complement each other. To a certain extent this still stands and it's a good place to start, particularly if you are eating authentic regional food. However, as our world becomes smaller, the regional nature of cooking and winemaking has become a bit fuzzier. Winemakers all over the world are adopting a fresher, more fruit-driven style of winemaking and chefs often make dishes blending more than one style of food or flavours. So don't get too hung up on where it comes from and think about the flavours instead.

Sweet is not necessarily sweet enough. Dessert wines are a bit tricky and many people just miss them out, unsure of what to get and what to do with the leftovers. The general rule is to aim for a wine that is a tiny bit sweeter than your pud – don't worry, the acidity in a good dessert wine (sometimes known as a 'sticky') should clear your palate so your mouth isn't left too sugary. In terms of leftover sweet wines (something I don't struggle with that much), have them instead of pudding or check out some of the cheese-matching recommendations.

CHEESE

Cheese is so like wine – each one is slightly different depending on the producer, the provenance and even the vintage. As the texture, acidity, consistency and flavours of the cheese change, so the perfect wine match changes too. My advice is go for what you like – the cheese will manage and you'll be happy.

Contrary to popular belief, you don't have to drink big reds or port with cheese: a lot of white wines work even better. If you are doing a big set-piece dinner, make like the Europeans and have your cheeseboard before dessert. That way you can graze between your dinner wines and your dessert wines to go with the cheese.

- Light and creamy goat's cheese – try Sauvignon Blanc, particularly Sancerre, or chilled reds like Cabernet Franc from the Loire.
- Hard ewe's cheese (e.g. Manchego) – sherry is a particularly good match (try Amontillado or Oloroso) or a softer red wine like Valpolicella.
- Semi-hard cheese (e.g. Gruyere, Comté) – you need some acidity here, so try Sauvignon Blanc or even Riesling from New Zealand, or perhaps a New World Pinot Noir.
- Hard strong cheese (e.g. Cheddar) – traditional reds work best, although you do need some ripe flavours – try an Australian Shiraz or Languedoc, or crack open some Port!
- Blue cheese – port or a sweet wine like Sauternes or Monbazillac work beautifully.

○ Pungent soft cheese (e.g. Camembert) – try a sweet wine like Monbazillac, or perhaps an aromatic white like Gewürztraminer.

CHINESE FOOD

Chinese food is not always easy to pair wine with: the use of sweet and sour flavours and tendency towards slightly oilier dishes can leave wine quaking in its boots. It's interesting that until very recently wine wasn't produced in China so there isn't a traditional 'local' option.

○ With white wine go for the aromatic styles with acidity and a hint of sweetness. Riesling, Viognier and Gewürztraminer are all good starting points.
○ For a red wine, Carmenère is a good all-rounder, as are Merlot and Zinfandel. It's worth noting that a good-quality Shiraz can set a crispy duck pancake roll off a treat.

Don't discount rosé wine with Chinese food. The halfway house between red and white with good acidity and some fruit and spice really works. Avoid the sweet 'blush' style wines and look for something Spanish or from the New World – or for a real treat try Pink Champagne with dim sum!

COMFORT FOOD

Imagine this: your kitchen is warm and cosy, you've had a long day, your feet are tired and your soul needs soothing. You open the saucepan lid, the windows steam up and there it is, your holy grail. Mashed potato! Accompanying this heaven-sent food is a little package of loveliness – maybe sausages or a pastry-topped pie. It's not hard to do these dishes justice with a good wine match.

Bangers and mash

Try Australian Shiraz, Côtes du Rhône, Chilean Merlot, Carmenère or Fitou from the Languedoc – what you're looking for is big and fruity with some spice and structure. If you can't bear switching white to red even for bangers and mash then opt for some Chenin Blanc, unoaked Chardonnay or Fiano. Or hedge your bets and have some spicy New World Rosé.

Pies

- O Chicken and ham or mushroom pie – Pinot Noir, Chardonnay and red or white Rioja
- O Steak and kidney pie – Bordeaux or Malbec
- O Pork pie – Fitou from the Languedoc
- O Fish pie – lighter, less smoky pies could happily pair up with crisp wines like Rueda, Sauvignon Blanc and New World Semillon. More smoky dishes require more body, so try a Viognier or oaked Chenin Blanc.

CURRY

Curry is such a broad term, covering all manner of dishes and ways of eating. The style of curry cuisine changes significantly as you travel through India and South-east Asia, ranging from hot, dry tandoori to creamy, coconut-based Malaysian curries.

Lightly spiced dishes

With dishes that don't blow your head off, aromatic white wines are a good option. Their inherent sweetness offsets the heat and the slightly richer texture complements the creamier sauces of Thai and Malay food. Riesling and Gewürztraminer are able to manage a good dose of aromatic spices as well as most meats and fishes as principal ingredients.

With Thai prawns or fishcakes you could go to the light end of both the Aromatic and White Central lines to Pinot Gris, Vinho Verde and Grüner Veltliner. The flavours tend to be lighter and the wines a bit crisper than the more aromatic wines, which can complement the flavours without being overpowering.

Red wine seems to go surprisingly well with certain curries. Not eye-watering Vindaloo or Madras, but savoury southern and north Indian curries, with garam masala, cumin, coriander seeds and curry leaves. Carmenère from Chile has an earthy note that ties in with those flavours and makes a head-turning match. Other reds worth trying are Carignan from the south of France and Montepulciano d'Abruzzo.

For bigger, hotter dishes
You need to accept that this is tricky and you might be better off with a glass of milk! However, there are some principles that will help.

Refreshing whites don't do much refreshing if the food is spicy! Overt acidity is the killer – try opting for something softer with a hint of sweetness.

Reds might work, depending how hot the curry is! As before Carmenère, Carignan or Montepulciano are good options. Avoid high alcohol and highly tannic wines.

Rosé can do well, as long as it's big and bold with some sweetness. Syrah rosé from California would be a good choice. Pink Fizz from the New World has an extraordinary effect when paired with hot curries – it's not to everyone's taste, but it's worth trying.

DESSERTS

Dessert wine, stickies, sweet wine, pudding wine: call it what you will, but dessert wine seems to hold a bit of scary mystery and many people prefer to steer clear of it altogether. It's certainly not for everyday drinking, nor is it cheap. However, it has a cult following in the food and wine trade – with good reason – you just need to give it a go!

The main rule of dessert wine is that it should be at least as sweet if not a little sweeter than what you're eating. You should also think about the texture, as you don't want to drown your pudding but neither do you want anything over sticky with it. If you love pudding, here are some matches made in sweet-tooth heaven.

Light and fruity

From fruit salads to perfumed meringues, if you've got a light and frothy dessert then you need something sweet but not too sticky. Try lightly sparkling Moscato or off-dry Prosecco for the gentle sweetness and froth. For a more sophisticated match I love the delicate Spätlese or Auslese Rieslings from Germany or Austria, which balance a semi-sweet and perfumed nature with a clean acidity, leaving you with no heavy sweetness.

Cakes

There are a tranche of lighter cakes like panettone or madeleines that sometimes pop up as dessert (or even just elevenses) and might require a glass of something lovely. My first call is fizz – demi-sec Champagne or semi-seco Cava have just a touch of sweetness and aren't too fruity to go with cake. It's the perfect afternoon tea fizz, which also goes with strawberries extremely well. A lightly fortified Muscat de Beaumes-de-Venise can do very nicely, particularly with denser almond-based cakes.

Dessert wine is a generic term for wines that people drink with dessert, i.e. sweet wines. I break it down into three distinct groups:

Fizz – ranging from very soft, simple, grapey sweet wines like Moscato to the intense sweet Champagnes.

Late Harvest – grapes that have been left to ripen on the vine much longer than normal in order to become intensely ripe and therefore produce sweeter wines.

Concentrated grapes – in order to intensify the flavours various techniques are used to extract water from the grape and leave a more intense, sticky juice.

○ In cold climates the grapes are left on the vine to freeze, which takes a lot of the water content out of the grape, leaving the sweet juice. These ice wines or Eisweins usually come from high-latitude vineyards, typically Germany, Austria and Canada. They are really rare.

○ In warm climates the grapes are picked and laid out to dry until they are almost raisins, and the little juice left is rich, sticky and intense. The most famous of these is a Spanish wine called Pedro Ximenez or PX, which is so sweet it's often mixed with other wines to dilute it.

○ Some of the most intense sweet wines are created when grapes develop a condition called Botrytis or Noble Rot. This happens in vineyards when the climate is moist but not too wet. The 'rot' sucks away at the water leaving only a little juice remaining, with a specific honey flavour. It is impossible to force this 'noble rot' to happen, and the risk is that the other kind of not-so-good rot turns up instead. I know it all sounds horrible but the wines made from botrytised grapes are incredibly special. The most famous wines made with these grapes are Sauternes and Tokaji, which are sought after all over the world.

Citrus, fresh fruit tarts and cheesecakes

As soon as you start getting into pastry, creams and fruit you need a wine that has more body and is zestier than the softer options. New World late-harvest wines, like Sauvignon Blanc and Riesling, work really well. I particularly like Chilean and New Zealand late-harvest Riesling: it has a zingy flavour that really works with desserts like lemon cheesecake. For berries and summer fruits look for something like a sweet German Riesling, Auslese, Beerenauslese or Trockenbeerenauslese.

Crumbles and pies

This category of dessert requires some serious wine. A good option is a wine that has had some botrytis for its honey flavours. The greatest sweet wines, like Sauternes and Tokaji, are made like this but you do pay a premium for the name. You can get better value from the lesser-known French Monbazillac (from the Loire) and botrytised wines from the southern hemisphere. Look for the terms 'Noble Rot' or 'Botrytis' on the back label. These wines really work with baked fruit and heavier pastries as well as the obligatory custard or cream.

Chocolate

It is notoriously difficult to match wine to chocolate, yet for many people it is the perfect double indulgence. For lighter chocolate desserts like chocolate mousse try the sweet, sparkling red Brachetto d'Acqui which, like Moscato d'Asti, is frizzante and lower in alcohol. For darker, more intense chocolate try late-harvest Black Muscat, which is dark pink with a musky exotic nose and velvety fruit. For really big chocolate desserts, Grenache-based fortified wines like Maury or the heavier Rivesaltes work wonderfully. For chocolate truffles and petit fours a botrytised sweet wine like Sauternes works best.

If you just fancy a square of chocolate there are some interesting matches to be made – the key is in starting with good chocolate made with cocoa butter and not oil – this prevents the chocolate coating your mouth with oil and ruining the wine.

- White chocolate – soft whites and pinks; the best match is Moscato d'Asti with white chocolate covered in freeze-dried raspberries. Avoid very crisp, dry wines.
- Milk chocolate – soft reds, particularly New World Pinot Noir and some rosés. Avoid heavy tannins or very dry wines.
- Dark chocolate – bigger reds but preferably fortified wines and rich sherry: Oloroso with nutty chocolate is heavenly!

The really intense, dark stickies made by drying the grapes until they are like raisins are brilliant poured over vanilla ice cream like sauce. They are too sweet to drink on their own, unless you have teeth of steel.

One last thing – an amazing combination for sticky toffee pudding is Rutherglen Muscat, an intensely raisin-sweet wine from Australia. The two were made to be together.

MEDITERRANEAN FLAVOURS
Who can resist the beautiful colours and scents of a Mediterranean diet? With wine matching, in this case, the local rule of thumb definitely seems to work best.

- There's a wealth of red wines from the Languedoc that pair nicely with those herby flavours of the south of France. Try Fitou, Corbières or Minervois – they have lots of ripe fruit but enough acidity to deal with tomatoes, herbs and meat.

- Mediterranean white wines are also hard to beat – my favourites are Viognier, Muscat and Picpoul de Pinet. Other great options would be Albariño, Grüner Veltliner and of course some lovely juicy Sauvignon Blanc. Mediterranean food can be quite pungent so it needs a wine with similar pungency and good acidity.
- The Mediterranean is a hotbed of rosé wine, ranging from some so pale they're known as 'gris' to an intensely dark pink which will knock your socks off. Drink pale pink for aperitifs and nibbles, while the big rosés will do a great job with meats and strong, herby flavours.

PASTA

Where to begin with pasta? There's so much choice! If you follow the food rules then you have to look at things like acidity, weight and sweetness to direct you. With pasta, like pizza, there are some potential booby traps along the way – cream, chilli and lashings of melted mozzarella to name but a few.

Robust and rustic

Here you need a wine that is also rustic and robust and can handle tomatoes, meat and a handful of herbs. Big Italian reds work well – Amarone if you're splashing out, Valpolicella if you're not – and Languedoc reds like Fitou or Minervois are also a good bet. White-wise it's definitely trickier. You could try something like Fiano or the fail-safe Chardonnay, both of which have lots of body.

Carbonara, mushroom and cream

These tend to be earthy, savoury flavours of smoky pancetta, umami mushrooms or the breadcrumbs and Parmesan that often make their way in to these dishes. Good wine options are lighter reds like Pinot Noir, Barbera or Cabernet Franc, round whites like Viognier and actually some rosés such as Côtes de Provence or Cerasuolo (a dry wine from Montepulciano). Dry, salty sherry also goes brilliantly with intensely mushroomy and bacony dishes.

Light and winey

Whether it's seafood linguine, prawn and pea risotto or salmon with dill sauce, which all hinge on a blend of sweet seafood or fish, a hint of garlic, a bright green herb and a generous glug of white wine in the sauce, they can be tricky to match as you need to support rather than overwhelm them. It's very tricky to pick a red for these, but if pushed I'd opt for some soft Beaujolais. White-wise, go for slightly neutral medium-acidity whites like Gavi, Albariño or Chenin Blanc.

PICNICS

Who doesn't love taking some simple food into the sunshine and enjoying the liberation of eating al fresco? When it comes to the wine, simplicity and facility must prevail. You need to take a bottle with a screwcap (no need for a corkscrew!) or even a box of wine if there are lots of you. Don't go for whites that need to be enjoyed chilled, like Vinho Verde or Pinot Grigio, unless you are certain you can keep them cold. Instead take something with a bit more fruit and body from further into the WineTubeMap, which will fare better if they aren't freezing cold. For the same reason I would opt for softer, juicier reds like Beaujolais, Valpolicella or some of the Languedoc reds like Fitou. They will fare better at a variety of temperatures and with a variety of foods.

PIZZA

The challenge with pizza is that it comes in so many different formats and with absolutely anything on top. The weight and flavour can change dramatically and therefore so can the wine that you pair it with. That said, pizza normally represents a night chilling out in front of the TV or a convivial night out in the local Italian restaurant, which means you shouldn't break into a sweat or break the bank when you're trying to decide what to buy.

Classic matches

You can't beat an inexpensive Italian red with any kind of pizza – the combination of juicy fruit, soft tannins and acidity really work. Valpolicella and pizza are a match made in heaven. On the white side, go for a juicy New World number with a bit of body to cope with all the elements, and a bit of oak helps with the wood-fired character. Try something like a softly wooded Australian Chardonnay.

Experimental choices

Keep the theme of soft tannins and fruit but add some bubbles with either a sparkling pink or red wine – make sure you're in the medium category, as bone-dry or sweet won't work. Who said pizza night can't be a bit of a celebration? You could also try something a bit more fragrant like a Viognier, which has the combination of body and flavour to match the pizza.

RISOTTO

Creamy, warming, comforting or sophisticated – like pasta, risotto is a relatively neutral base when it comes to food matching, as almost all of the flavour comes from what you do (and don't do) to those pearly grains of rice. It's not a shrinking violet, however, and the creamy nature means you do need some acidity and body so you don't lose your wine!

Mushroom risotto

White

White Burgundy works well because it generally has enough body to stand up to the creamy nature and, unlike some Chardonnays, the fruity character is more subtle. You don't have to go for the most expensive one though – look for premium own-label Burgundy or Saint-Véran. Otherwise head for something Italian and a bit esoteric: Fiano and Falanghina both have a wonderful nuttiness.

Rosé

Côtes de Provence is a real winner here – its subtlety really shines with mushroomy, garlicky dishes.

Red

If the budget stretches, the intensely savoury Barolo is an amazing choice, leading mushroom risotto into the deepest, darkest autumn night! Otherwise Pinot Noir (ideally from Burgundy for the same reason as the Chardonnay) works fabulously. If budget doesn't quite stretch there, stick with Italian wine: something like Barbera (one of the grapes that makes up Barolo) is much more reasonably priced and does a good job.

Light risottos

Many risottos have a hint of sweetness, brought by the addition of ingredients like peas or crème fraiche. A lightness of touch is needed here. New Zealand Sauvignon Blanc is an option, as is Grüner Veltliner, Rueda or Gavi. You can definitely experiment with rosés with a hint of ripe fruit, like the Grenache rosés or some lighter New World rosés.

Smoky risottos

If your risotto is pancetta-heavy or even contains some smoked salmon you might need to head back to some slightly more savoury wines – Pinot Noir, Chianti, White Rioja or some Italian whites like Fiano and Falanghina will all balance the smokiness.

ROAST DINNERS

Pork and chicken

These are the 'lighter' end of roasts, where you can easily drink red or white wine. Both meats have quite firm pale flesh and a high oil content in the skin (or crackling – yum). Classically a buttery oaked Chardonnay from Burgundy or the New World provides a lovely rich accompaniment, particularly if you're using fresh flavours like lemon or thyme. For more savoury flavours and slow roasts try Semillon or the Italian whites like Fiano, both of which would work well with sage flavours and meaty stuffing. Lower-tannin reds will also work well to accompany these roasts: Chianti or Beaujolais Villages are great options.

Lamb

Lamb is tricky because of the high fat content; you need a wine that can refresh your palate, and that means you need acidity. The classic pairing is Pinot Noir either from Burgundy or New Zealand. Of the two, the Burgundy tends to have an earthier set of flavours, which goes well with garlic and rosemary rubs and slow roasts. The New World styles have more fruit flavours so can enhance minty marinades and pinker meat.

Beef

Here you need structure and a certain sense of occasion. Go
for some Bordeaux, ideally Supérieur or better still some
Médoc. This can handle a big slab of roast beef, Yorkshire
puddings and some serious gravy. This is an excuse for some
blockbuster reds, so if you don't want Bordeaux try good
Cabernet Sauvignon, Rioja or Malbec.

Veggie roasts

With these earthy vegetable flavours – and often a sprinkling of
cheese – it's safe to err towards the wine choices that match
pork and chicken. Try Chardonnay, Semillon or even some
Riesling, or Italian reds like Chianti or Valpolicella Ripasso.

SEAFOOD

Shellfish

You can't go wrong here with a glass of bubbly. A classic
match for oysters is a crisp, clean Muscadet sur Lie made on
the French Atlantic coast and almost tasting of the sea. Vinho
Verde, Grüner Veltliner and Semillon are also great seafood
options – all have a citrus character which works a little like a
squeeze of lemon.

Prawns

Prawns on their own or with simple citrus flavours work fantas-
tically with New Zealand Sauvignon Blanc or New World
Rieslings. Chilli and spicy flavours require some sweetness –
Rieslings, Gewürztraminer and Pinot Grigio provide this while
maintaining some acidity. Prawns in tomato sauce can pair
nicely with Italian reds or chilled-down Cabernet Francs.

Mussels

Moules-frîtes was previously the domain of the Belgians and French seaside towns but now mussels pop up everywhere as a cheap and sustaining meal. This means the simple white wine and garlic sauce is often jazzed up with Thai or curry flavours, tomatoes or paprika. You can drink a range of wines with these, from classic Chablis to Viognier, Pinot Gris and Riesling. If you prefer reds then, as with the prawns, choose a wine with low tannins and reasonable acidity.

Smoked salmon

You can't veer too far from something sparkly here. If your budget doesn't stretch to Champagne, try something like Crémant d'Alsace or Crémant de Bourgogne, both are cheaper alternatives. Pinot Noir is also a surprisingly good match for smoked salmon: it works incredibly well with the smoky, oily fish (as it's one of the constituent grapes of Champagne, perhaps it's not that much of a surprise).

White fish

Monkfish, pollock, hake and cod (sustainably fished, of course) all make up a large part of our fishy dinners. Because the fish themselves are quite neutral you need to focus your wine choice on the flavours that go with the fish. As a general rule White Rioja, Fiano, Chenin Blanc and Chardonnay would all work well. With smoked fish, look for something oak-aged to complement the smoky flavour. If the dish is lighter, the citrussy Semillon, Sauvignon Blanc and Rueda will work nicely, as would Albariño.

Oily fish

With oily fish like salmon and mackerel, go for a zingy but off-dry style of white wine. Riesling, Semillon and Pinot Blanc all have the right balance.

Fish and chips / fish fingers
It might sound a bit indulgent to open a bottle of wine for these, but why wouldn't you want to enhance a sneaky fish finger sandwich or fish and chips? Particularly as fish and chips are part of some of life's big moments: they are, for example, obligatory food for house moves. Which is obviously why Champagne is such a perfect match for fish and chips, particularly very dry Champagnes like the newly marketed Zero Dosage. Fish finger sandwich? Go for New Zealand Sauvignon, which has enough acidity to go with ketchup and enough green flavours to be your tartare sauce.

TAPAS
Tapas covers everything from Spanish omelette and cheese to roasted peppers and gherkins to *albondigas* (meatballs), *jamón* and calamari. And it's not just Spanish dishes these days either – there are often lovely little Indian and Thai additions, making for a real feast. With all of that choice you need a wine that plays the role of best supporting actor, delivering the goods without trying too hard. After all, a tapas night is about conviviality, not necessarily sophistication.

With robust tapas, open a bottle of Rioja or Ribera del Duero. If it's a bit lighter try Valpolicella or Côtes du Rhone. If you prefer white wine, Albariño makes a great accompaniment, as do Rueda or Sauvignon Blanc. Navarra Rosé, rich but not sweet, is a lovely alternative, as are a lot of gutsy New World rosés. To top it all off if you are having a celebration then a dry Cava or Crémant d'Alsace would add some bubbles that don't fade away with all those flavours.

THAI

Thai food is tricky to match with wine: the blend of sweet, salty, sour and spicy makes it challenging to find a wine that doesn't just curl up and disappear or lose any sense of balance. If you were to follow the 'drink what the locals drink' rule, you would probably be drinking jasmine or green tea rather than a glass of wine! However, it's not impossible, and as with everything, drinking something you like is a good start, even if it isn't the perfect match.

○ The case for off-dry white wines is strong with Thai food: Riesling, Pinot Gris and Gewürztraminer all tend to shine. The combination of aromatics, spiciness and a hint of sweetness work well with the Thai flavours and coconut creaminess. A fabulous, low-cost all-rounder is the incredibly fragrant Viña Esmeralda. Made from a blend of Gewürztraminer and Moscatel, it's great with a mixture of lighter dishes.

○ For zingy salads and fishcakes, Sauvignon Blanc and Semillon make a good showing, particularly the Semillon if it is a couple of years old. Other great options are something sparkling: Champagne and Cava work really well with fried food, so it's a great pairing with starter sharing platters, but dry Champagne can't stand up to chilli heat so don't pair it with spicy dishes.

○ The slightly sweeter New World rosés can do a good job, and with a good balance between the fruit and acidity, some of the pink sparklers are worth a try. For reds, avoid the big tannic wines, which don't work with chilli, and instead head for Beaujolais or a soft Italian or southern French wine like Barbera or Carignan.

Food Matching 135

Troubleshooting Wine

Modern winemaking techniques have reduced or even eradicated faults that you used to find in wines and there are very few bad wines on the shelves these days. But some problems can occur even with the most carefully made wine. If you do have a problem with a bottle then you are completely within your rights to return it to where you bought it with the receipt and they should replace the bottle. The same goes for restaurants and bars, although be prepared to stand your ground.

The symptoms	The fault	The solution
Musty, mouldy-smelling wine Lower end of the scale – dull flavours and no fruitiness. Upper end of the scale – wet cardboard, rotting leaves, musty-smelling wine. Seriously not nice.	**Corked wines / TCA taint** The term 'corked' actually refers to the presence of a compound in wine called TCA. This compound has a detrimental effect on the flavour of the wine. It occurs most frequently in corks, although can be found in other parts of the winemaking process, meaning a wine bottled in a screwcap could technically be corked.	☹ **Send it back** There is, however, a school of thought that you can lose the taint by performing a trick with a plastic bowl and cling film (look it up on YouTube!).
Bits in your wine Cork	This is not corked wine: occasionally the cork crumbles when you open the bottle.	☺ **Keep it** (and pick the bits out)
Crystals	Sometimes crystals form in wine at cool temperatures, particularly if the wine hasn't been heavily filtered – these are not harmful at all.	☺ **Carefully decant the wine and the crystals should stay in the bottle.**
Sediment	In older red wines sediment can form as the elements age. Again totally harmless (although not nice to drink).	☺ **Carefully decant the wine and the sediment should stay in the bottle.**

The symptoms	The fault	The solution
Glass and other foreign bodies	Clearly this should not happen and could be dangerous.	☹ Send it back **Try to take all the packaging (cork/ screwcap) back with the bottle.**
A light fizz or prickly bubbles in the bottle when it's not a sparkling wine (or Vinho Verde)	**Refermentation** Very occasionally a secondary fermentation (a bit like Champagne) can take place where leftover yeast and sugar react. As the aim isn't for a sparkling wine this is a fault!	☹ Send it back **Try to take all the packaging (cork/ screwcap) back with the bottle.**
Wine has taken on a brown colour (this happens in red, white or rosé wines) and the wine has lost its fresh smells and flavours, taking on a Madeira-like, caramel smell.	**The wine is oxidised** Somehow the wine has been exposed to oxygen, which has broken down the structure and fruit components, leaving you with something altogether flat and unpleasant.	☹ Send it back **Try to take all the packaging (cork/ screwcap) back with the bottle.**
Wine smells like vinegar and is undrinkable.	**Acetic acid** The wine has an excess of volatile acidity where a problem leads to some of the alcohol being converted into acetic acid (the acid you find in vinegar).	☹ Send it back **Try to take all the packaging (cork/ screwcap) back with the bottle.**

The symptoms	The fault	The solution
The wine smells like burnt matches, rotten eggs and might make you sneeze.	**There is some sulphur dioxide lurking!** This is used to prevent the wines becoming oxidised but can sometimes hang around.	☺ This should 'blow off' once the wine is opened, so decant it, give it a swirl and see. If it doesn't seem to change – Send it back!
The wine seems to be a bit dull and rather than tasting fresh fruit flavours you can taste over-ripe fruits or even no fruit at all. The acidity is low and the wine is a bit thin.	**Past its best** You need to check your facts, but it might be that the wine is just past its best. Check the vintage and back label: if the label says consume within 6 or 12 months then the wine is made to be drunk as soon as possible.	☺ If you've recently bought the wine and it's past that recommendation then take it back. If you've been saving it then more fool you!

The WineTubeMap®

Some Advanced Manoeuvres

You've read the book, you've tempted your taste buds with wines similar to your favourites and you're hungry for more, so what next?

Host a wine party
Invite some of your friends around and do some comparing and contrasting. Nothing teaches you more about wine than trying two next to each other and literally tasting the difference.

- Pick a section of the WineTubeMap and 4-6 wines from it
- Ask your guests to bring a different variety of wine - and set a budget so no one feels hard done by
- Pour a sample of each into a different glass (unless you have an endless supply of glasses), put a sticker on each glass with the name or number of the wine on it
- Try the wines in WineTubeMap order and note the differences - which ones you like, don't like and why
- Pick your favourite and have a glass with some nibbles and generally put the world to rights
- Why not make it a regular thing? It's a great way to explore the Tube Map and learn more about wine

BYOB at home

Next time you're ordering a take away dinner or cooking a feast for friends, look at the wine-matching recommendations for that type of food and buy (or get your friends to bring) a selection of the options. Pour samples of each wine and see which ones go best with which foods – you'll be amazed how everyone has an opinion and how helpful it is next time you're in a restaurant. This is how I did a lot of the testing of the food-matching recommendations in the book – much to my friends' and family's delight!

Plan your wine journey

Once you've sampled the wines around your tried and tested favourites, plot yourself a more adventurous route and gradually work your way through. Look out for your selected wines going on promotion, or buy them when there is a 25% off all wine deal in one of the supermarkets. It's a great way to build up your wine repertoire.

Index

Acknowledgements

The WineTubeMap would not exist without its co-creator and my partner in wine, Ged, who has unwaveringly supported me from the seed of an idea to its fruition. Thank you for putting up with the delayed trains and service interruptions.

And who knows whether a trip to the World Wine Fair aged two was the catalyst for my wine obsession? Either way, I have my Mum and Dad to thank for making sure I always mind the gap and that my glass is full rather than empty.

Thanks to the Trium, for your endless encouragement and blatant promotion, but mostly for being on the train with me. And Mini, who put up with the daily messages – 'Just checking something'!

Margaret and Jim Cuthbert put me in touch with Birlinn with whom I've really enjoyed working. They have translated the concept into a great little book. Graham at Project transformed the map into something beautiful for me and consistently gets it. Thanks, G!

Over the years I've met some amazing people in the wine world who have inspired me with their patience, kindness, ability to party hard and to make awesome wines. And during the last couple of years so many people have come to the WineTubeMap events and tastings and given us support, suggestions and general wine loveliness. Without you all I wouldn't have wanted to do this.

Cheers, people!

Nikki Welch

Amarone

Valpolicella

Beaujolais

Chianti

New World Rose

White Zinfandel

Red Fizz

Pink Fiz

Grenache
/ Garnacha Rosé

Côtes
de Provence

Demi-sec
/ Semi-seco

Prosecco

Muscat

Cava

Moscato

Non Vint
Champa

Gewürztraminer

Traditional
method

Viognier

Fiano

Chardon

Riesling

Gavi

White Rioja

Albariño

Chenin Blanc

Rueda

Grüner Veltliner

Sauvignon Blanc

M

Vinho Verde

Semillon

Pinot Gris

Pinot Grigio